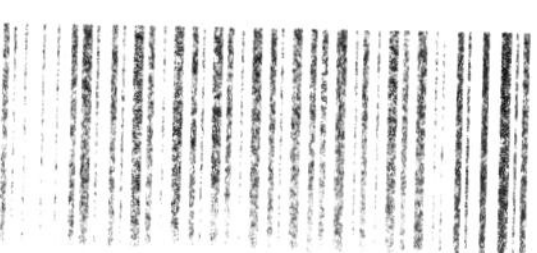

Time Off to Learn

TIME OFF to LEARN

Paid educational leave and low-paid workers

Edited by Jane Mace and Martin Yarnit

METHUEN

First published in 1987 by
Methuen & Co. Ltd
11 New Fetter Lane, London EC4P 4EE

Published in the USA by
Methuen & Co.
in association with Methuen, Inc.
29 West 35th Street, New York NY 10001

Typeset by Graphicraft Typesetters Ltd., Hong Kong

Printed and Bound in Great Britain by Biddles Ltd,
Guildford and King's Lynn

British Library Cataloguing in Publication Data

Time off to learn: paid educational leave
and low-paid workers.
1. Educational leave — Europe
2. Adult education — Europe
I. Mace, Jane II. Yarnit, Martin
331.25'763 HD5257.2.E8

ISBN 0-416-02102-6

Contents

Foreword

A thriving democracy with cultural wealth and economic health requires a system of education which provides for an aware and educated population; a population continuously engaged in developing their full potential as individuals as well as raising their skills base and extending their vocational opportunities.

The current system of compulsory education has failed to meet the needs of most citizens and has particularly failed those who find themselves in low-paid manual jobs.

Provision for imaginative vocational education and training and second chance adult and continuing education is almost non-existent. Consequently those who have been let down by compulsory provision up to 16 years of age, have few opportunities for improving their life chances thereafter.

Recent developments in Manpower Services Commission provision have given further cause for concern, particularly where Local Education Authority control of further education has been eroded in order to provide short-term, employer-led training for skills which may not be required in the longer term.

The trades union movement has a responsibility to campaign industrially and politically for policies and legislation which will ensure that its members, their families and the disadvantaged who are outside our organizations are provided with opportunities to remedy the failure of both the compulsory and the vocational education systems to meet their needs.

High-quality vocationally oriented education and training is essential if we are to have an efficient, productive and motivated working population capable of making choices about where and how they earn their living, and trade unions should seek to negotiate with employers for imaginative and practical schemes of in-service education and training. However, negotiations cannot substitute for effective government action enabling all employees to have opportunities for developing their skills base.

Provision has also to be made for the unemployed and other disadvantaged groups to bring them into employment and into the mainstream of cultural activity. It is not without significance that in 1985/6, in the midst of mass unemployment, the Department of Education and Science spent £3.5 million on education provision for the adult unemployed. A matter of only £1 per head of the 'revised' unemployment figures.

Second-chance adult and continuing education must be given a higher priority by government than hitherto. Without access to learning opportunities the disadvantaged will live without hope. Access, however, does not only mean how people get into educational institutions but also how we take educational experience into the community.

Separate provision must be made for release with pay for trade union education. The provisions of the Employment Protection Act are limited to begin with but have been steadily eroded even further through employer resistance. Legislation will have to be argued for which will provide access, without financial penalty, to trade union education for both representatives and members.

However, imaginative employer-resourced schemes of 'in-service' education of the kind referred to in some of the case studies in this book must not be confused with paid educational leave for genuinely free choices, to be made by individuals, about the form and content of the adult and continuing education they may wish to pursue. Neither must it be allowed to be 'offset' against entitlement to participate in trade union education controlled by the trade union movement.

A great deal has still to be done if effective policies and legislation are to be achieved in this area of educational provision. Such policies and legislation will not emerge without an informed debate and effective campaigning.

This book makes a useful contribution to that process.

Rodney K. Bickerstaffe
General Secretary
National Union of Public Employees

Contributors

GRAHAM BIRKIN has taught in schools, colleges and adult education since the early 1970s. He now works on Take Ten, Sheffield.

STEVE BOND also teaches on Take Ten. He has researched and written on Sheffield's local economy and local government.

ANNA BRASOLIN teaches English on a 150 Hours course in Bologna, Italy. She has worked on the scheme since its early years.

CATHY BURKE, as well as teaching on Take Ten, is a musician, and secretary of Sheffield Women's History Group.

PETER CALDWELL is a trade union education tutor for the Workers' Educational Association (WEA) in Coventry.

MICHAEL CUNNINGHAM, a NUPE full-time official, has taken a particular interest in negotiating paid release for workers for education and training. He has written and contributed to a number of books on trade unionism, including *Non-Wage Benefits* (Pluto Press, 1981).

JUDITH EDWARDS has taught for the last twenty years in the UK and abroad in a variety of settings. She has spent the last six years with Second Chance to Learn, Liverpool, teaching and developing techniques for evaluating educational provision.

DAVE EVA, currently senior lecturer at South Mersey College, Liverpool, has worked in trade union education for the last decade. He is joint author (with Ron Oswald) of *Health and Safety at Work* (Pan, 1981).

EILEEN KELLY has worked on Second Chance to Learn since 1977, teaching and developing materials. She has made a key contribution to establishing working-class women's history groups and research.

JANE MACE has worked in adult literacy since 1970 and is head of Lee Community Education Centre, Goldsmiths' College, London.

She is the author of *Working with Words: literacy beyond school* (Writers and Readers, 1979).

MAGGIE NORTON is a tutor with Take Ten. She also teaches yoga. Previously, she worked with Women's Aid.

LIZ SMITH is a lecturer in trade union studies at South Mersey College, Liverpool. Formerly a WEA tutor-organizer with special responsibility for the unemployed, she is a founder member, former president and current vice-president of Merseyside Trade Union, Community and Unemployed Resource Centre.

SONIA VILLONE has worked in adult education in Bologna, Italy for ten years. Her involvement with the 150 Hours scheme goes back to the early 1970s when it began.

MARY WOLFE has taught PEL (paid educational leave) courses in London since 1978. She has been a member of the staff of Workbase since 1983.

MARTIN YARNIT lives in Sheffield and works for the City Council. The co-founder of Second Chance to Learn in Liverpool, he has written about it and Italy's 150 Hours in Jane Thompson's *Adult Education for a Change* (Hutchinson, 1980).

Introduction

Jane Mace and Martin Yarnit

This is a book about work and pleasure. It's also, like most writing and talk which deals with the realities of an unequal society, about difficulty and struggle. As for us, the fourteen people who wrote it, we have one thing in common: all of us, in one way or another, are employed as negotiators for other people's education. The contradiction with which we work is this: we ourselves have both qualifications and employment, yet the women and men who become our students often have neither. 'Paid educational leave' (PEL), the theme of this book, is one of the few means by which, as we see it, such differentials can be challenged. It is a means to redress educational inequality. Leave for education which has been negotiated with, rather than 'on behalf of' oppressed groups is also, we suggest, about liberating personal and collective strengths. It therefore has political implications. The trade union movement has known for a long time the importance of education as a means for such individual and social change. We believe that this knowledge needs reaffirming, and that leave for study of this kind, in conditions which remove economic pressures, needs to become once again central to a demand for humane and co-operative conditions of employment. We argue, too, that the commitment by the trade union movement to campaigns for unemployed people, and to working-class people who do not happen to be paid-up members, is enriched and strengthened by this claim for the 'time off to learn'.

A domestic or a porter, a nursing auxiliary or a home help, a dustman or a care assistant, who routinely work in low status jobs often in irregular shifts, often part time, have little spare energy, time or money for their personal or collective development. The space and time to come together, with an educational purpose, on their own terms, in 'worktime', is work. It can also be an opportunity for enjoyment. For those who are unemployed or, as women, shouldering the unpaid jobs of childcare, housework, managing on low incomes, allowing themselves 'leave' for their own education can mean a release of energy and assertion that they had forgotten they had. All of this means that participants in such courses stand to gain, not only personal self-confidence, but also a sense of solidarity, and ideas for how to formulate demands for change. Education which aims to confront inequality, after all, is not an end in itself, but a means to change the conditions which produced that inequality in the first place.

Within the world of paid employment, the right to paid leave for workers to learn and study together for their own educational purposes, when it is won, will be an important sequel to those other hard-won rights of paid leave for workers' sickness, holidays and maternity (rights still denied, of course, to the large numbers of mainly female part-time employees). Until then, for the large majority of adults in this country, the contradiction remains: that while for 'professionals' (nearly always white, usually male) it is taken for granted that PEL is part of the job, for the large mass of other, low-paid workers, the chance to have time off their usual work for education or training is inconceivable.

A good image of this contrast was offered to some of us during the period of writing this book, when six Sheffield council workers and the four tutors of the PEL course which they had attended gave a workshop on the subject of PEL at the Annual Study Conference of the National Institute of Adult Continuing Education in Sheffield (in April 1986). Some 300 adult educationalists from all over the country were in residence that week, in university accommodation, on release from our usual workplaces, freed from our usual day-to-day deadlines, demands, pressures, unfinished tasks, and telephones. Those six people were being asked that afternoon to discuss what they felt they had gained from taking part, for the first time in their working lives, in a course of 40 or 60 hours, spread over ten weeks, on release from *their* usual jobs. Those of us who talked with them were in that building and at that conference on leave, effectively, for the same amount of time – within one week. Attending such conferences (usually for one or two days at a time) is assumed to be part of our job. Few of us there, however, would have seen ourselves to be on PEL. Why not? Because it is taken for granted that the stimulus and interchange of such events are necessary to our effectiveness as 'professionals'. It's our job to be there.

In Britain, public spending on education and training for adults is so arranged that the gap which yawns betwen two school-leavers, one without qualifications and the other who goes on to full-time study, grows wider and deeper as they grow older. PEL to us is not just a perk to be offered to more people in paid employment; it means 'payment for a period of leave for education' in the broadest sense, which should include unwaged women and men, and above all extend new possibilities for learning to the full range of adults. Our aim in this book has been to do two things: to draw attention to those continuing inequalities that exist in the opportunities for education and training; and to describe, within that context, such work that we know of which has begun, since 1976, to confront and challenge those inequalities. We who write are paid to work in jobs concerned with achieving adult education for working-class people and, for different reasons, we have all come to the conclusion that PEL is an indispensable mechanism for it to work. We don't pretend to come up with a single formula; and this is not a comprehensive survey of PEL. There are, for instance, no examples of PEL courses, other than for trade union education, offered to low-paid workers employed in the private sector. This is not because we have wanted to suggest that public employers have the monopoly of virtue. It is simply because we have been unable to discover the existence of any programmes, apart from one-off arrangements for individuals, having been successfully negotiated with private employers.[1]

In the first six chapters of this book we have tried to set out how, against persistent economic and social pressures to the contrary, a variety of radical educational and training initiatives have been created in recent years in Britain, in which women, black people, unemployed people and adult literacy students have been determining their own collective forms of learning. In the 'case studies' of Part II we have offered a more detailed history of four schemes of PEL study developed in the same period, picking out some of the problems they raise, as well as the new possibilities they suggest. Part III draws out, by way of summary, some of the experience of this work which could offer practical guidance to others wishing to negotiate for more such courses, and sets out the argument as to why any of this should be a central responsibility of the trade union movement as a whole.

When was it that PEL first appeared on any agenda for reform? And what is special about it, among any other socialist demands for change proposed over the years? The usual answer to the first question is: the ILO Convention 140, adopted by Britain in 1974. This book is our attempt to answer the second.

The ILO stands for the International Labour Organization. Set up in 1919 in accordance with the 'Versailles Treaty' after the First World War, its job was to help improve labour relations between member countries, and to build up an international code of fair practice. It was committed from the start to a policy of equal opportunities (and, at its first international conference held in Washington in 1919, conventions were produced on childbirth and maternity, children's employment, and on hours and shift work for women).[2] Convention 140, like all the others, had no legislative powers. John Killeen and Margaret Bird, who carried out the only national survey of paid educational leave in this country two years later (1976/7), pointed out that it had only the force of a 'vague consensus'.[3] As their report *Education and Work* made clear, the practice of PEL in this country is very far from expressive of even the most timid equal opportunities policy. Convention 140, after all, only asked that member states should 'formulate and apply a policy designed to promote, by methods appropriate to national conditions and practice, and by stages if necessary, the granting of paid educational leave'. PEL itself was defined broadly, as: 'leave granted to a worker for educational purposes for a specified period during working hours, with adequate financial entitlements'.

The key question, as so often, concerns the power to make those other definitions. Who shall have the power to define which 'educational purposes' are legitimate? How long shall a 'specified period' be? Who is to say what 'financial entitlements' are 'adequate'? Other European countries have devised a variety of answers to this.[4] From the experience of the '150 Hours' programme in Italy (of which one course in Bologna is described in detail in chapter 10), and from the much smaller-scale beginnings in this country, it seems clear to us that this is a central issue, and it's the one which we keep returning to throughout this book.

The Italian '150 Hours' programme, negotiated by trade unions, giving the right to leave from paid work to follow an adult education course, has fascinated British adult educationalists and trade unions for more than a decade. In 1982, the two of us, with six members of the Merseyside Paid Educational Leave group first met with Sonia Villone, Anna Brasolin and their colleagues in Bologna, on a two-week study tour to learn more about the scheme. It seems particularly good that this book has been able to include an up-to-date account of its practice. PEL is hard enough for low-paid workers to achieve at a time of full employment; with high unemployment, in Italy as here, an entitlement to have time for study takes on a new and more urgent meaning.

Later, in the summer and autumn of 1984, some of us gathered, first in Sheffield, then in London, to discuss ideas about the paid leave courses we worked with in this country. We talked of the idea of a conference. We met a couple of times more. Then we ran out of steam; it had become difficult simply to convene our own meetings (always on Saturdays).[5] A year later (in November 1985), the two of us met again, in Sheffield, to discuss ideas for putting a book together and seeking a publisher to support us. The result is what you are reading now. Between that conversation and a bound volume two years later we have, with our contributors, engaged in that particular combination of misery and delight that is entailed in trying to 'dig where you stand'.[6]

A fundamental principle in the courses we describe has been one of non-hierarchical, collaborative approaches to learning. In setting out to write a book about them we assumed we should follow the same policy, and the two of us who took on the job of co-ordinating the whole also took on a commitment to include writers and contributors in all the planning and drafting stages. In practice, of course, decisions have to be made against deadlines; and since we all lived long journeys apart (Sheffield, Liverpool, Coventry, North London, South London, and Bologna, Italy) there had to be some short cuts in the democratic process. We all shared, too, a similar commitment to consult with those who, as participants in these courses, had a firsthand experience to contribute to the argument in each chapter, and several of these were interviewed for the book. For chapter 2, a series of taped interviews were arranged with women who had been on the PEL courses in Sheffield, followed by a meeting with all of them to discuss the tape transcripts and the ideas each had raised. For other chapters in that first section, records of projects in which the authors had been personally concerned were reread and discussed again with colleagues. Many others contributed to the chapters in Part II. Mary Wolfe, writing about Workbase in London, interviewed a number of people who had been, as manual workers, students on the courses, and drew on their voices to put together her account. In quoting from these interviews, we have tried to ensure that the speakers know exactly the use to which their words are being put. We have resorted, when in doubt, to the usual convention and used full names of people quoted only when full permission was given.

Our editorial meetings (on Saturdays, as in 1984), were never long enough to explore the differences of view that came up or the doubts as to how things had been written. From the start, we were aware of one particular limitation to our writing: all of us are white. We have discussed, at a number of stages in the process of writing, the fact of our whiteness and the limits that puts on what we know and can write about. The result, as you will find, is that while every chapter has stressed the importance of women's experience, and separate provision which takes account of that, the equal importance of black people's claim to their own space, on the other hand, is not fully developed anywhere. The summary of many discussions which we had on this with our contributors and others is, roughly, as follows.

We live in a society which is structurally and institutionally racist. Black women and men in low-status jobs face double discrimination. It's clear that they must have the right to determine their own demands for education, free from the suggestions of white anti-racists like ourselves. A number of the black people who contributed to the interviews for this book and to the discussions in the courses described have put their own views on this (see chapters 2, 7 and 8). Equal opportunity programmes developed in the last few years (see chapters 2 and 3) are only a start of the process of combating racism to which, we suggest, PEL can make a significant contribution.

One last, and we think intriguing point: certification, for the British PEL courses we have written about, has not been on offer. The Italian scheme, by contrast, awards the equivalent of a 'leaving school certificate' to those who attend the '150 Hours' courses. The market value of this qualification has increased along with increased competition for jobs (see p. 136). Yet neither their course, nor those in this country which we have discussed, are limited to 'job training'. It may become increasingly important that adults who do not happen to possess O levels or other qualifications see in PEL an opening to acquire precisely those things. Meanwhile, it seems that an important attraction for many people who have taken part in these first courses has been the lack of a pressure to be tested, and a co-operative, rather than competitive mode of learning. Lucy, a library assistant in Sheffield, one of the group presenting the conference workshop in April 1986, spoke of the contrast she had experienced between the O and A level courses she had taken, as an adult, in her own time, at college, and the ten-week Take Ten course she had taken as a council worker:

> There was no reward, there's no certificate; they weren't saying you have this, and there you are, you're officially a lot cleverer than you were when you started it. There was none of that. It was just, 'Come along and express yourself'. . . . I enjoyed my O and A levels, I thought that was really great, you know, wonderful; but I got a bigger kick out of this, and I had nothing at the end of it; just the knowledge that there were quite a few people in Sheffield that felt exactly the same way as I do. . . . to be able to say something, and it to be valuable to report, and people want to hear it, did a lot of good.

There are many reasons that stop us, and others in similar work, making the time to record what has happened in the midst of trying to ensure that it goes on happening. In the end, what probably made all of us persist with the effort was an impulse that also propels others to join us on the educational opportunities we are paid to organize: the impulse to reflect on and share what we know in order that we and others may learn from it. We wrote the book, in short, in order to extend the discussion about the quality and inequalities of education with others, in the women's movement, in black organizations, in education, in unions, and anywhere else; so that the few gains which have been achieved may be improved on, and added to. In researching for it, we have sought out what others have written about PEL as well as interviewing people; and we hope that the notes and address list will be of use to others wanting to pursue the arguments further. As we suggest in the last chapter, both broad strategies and immediate initiatives are needed.

Part I
Themes and movements

1

Paid educational leave: problems and possibilities (1976–86)

Martin Yarnit

In 1976, after one or two false starts, Keith Jackson (now senior tutor at the Northern College) and I recruited the first intake of students to a social studies course based in Liverpool University's Institute of Extension Studies. The course, which we called 'Second Chance to Learn', was part time. It was also long (thirty weeks), and the content by no means lightweight (the causes and consequences of the decline of Merseyside). Yet neither then, nor now, ten years later, has there ever been a shortage of takers. In the main, they have been unwaged women and men; but from the beginning, too, there has been a consistent minority of wage earners. In chapter 9, Judith Edwards and Eileen Kelly describe how some of those employed students look back on the problems of attending the course. Few ever got approval for release. The only way of joining it, for many, was to take unpaid time off work – with a consequent price to pay on an already limited household budget. Those not in paid work, and particularly women not used to putting their own needs first, had to find the money to pay for fares, food and books. Homework asked of course students is particularly hard for women used to giving way to the needs of others in the family. As tutors, we had to learn to address these problems in order to make a course intended for working-class women and men genuinely responsive to their situations. We had to take arranging nursery places for students' children as seriously as writing the curriculum. We had, too, to begin to recognize the need to negotiate release from paid employment which could enable those in jobs to have the 'second chance' this course presented.

In 1979, some of us in Liverpool came together to discuss these issues, and identified three key priorities on which we should campaign. These were: to give greater attention to the needs of women, to confront our own racism as white teachers directing the curriculum, and to address the issue of paid educational leave. One practical outcome was the formation of the Merseyside Paid Educational Leave Group. This group of students and tutors decided we needed to look at existing models of Paid Educational Leave (PEL) for working-class adults. Since, outside of trade-union education, there was little we could find in this country to learn from, we decided to raise the funds to go and visit the one scheme which we already had some contact with, through my own previous research there: the '150 Hours' programme in Italy, by then six years old. With funds raised from a variety of sources, principally UNESCO, a group of us went in November 1982 for two weeks to Bologna and Milan. On our return we compiled a report which gave an account of our observations together with a set of campaign priorities which we suggested were necessary to achieve PEL in this country.[1] That activity brought together several of the contributors to this book, and put us in touch with others pursuing parallel lines of thought and action. Above all, it made clear that paid release, while not the only way of correcting the imbalance of educational opportunity in Britain, was an indispensable part of an overall means to that end.

In later chapters, we describe how in the ten years 1976–86, new PEL opportunities developed. In this one, I shall discuss the three strands which I see as having a major influence on these experiences: the effect of the economic crisis on employment and training in the mid-1970s; the prevailing imbalance of resources devoted to education for adults; and the advances in educational opportunities which, despite these conditions, have been achieved by a variety of alliances.

Economics, employment and training

The mid-1970s brought to an end an era of rising expectations and a rising curve of public spending. It was the Labour government of James Callaghan which, in return for a loan from the International Monetary Fund in 1976, imposed a ceiling on state spending for the remainder of its term of office. The 5 per cent wage limit, the other side of the housekeeping exercise, provoked an explosion of anger among low-paid workers in the Health Service and local government which led directly to the defeat of Labour in the 1979 General

Election. James Callaghan, speaking the same autumn of 1976 to the Labour Party Conference, revealed the extent of the break with the full employment policies of all governments, Labour and Conservative, since the 1940s.[2] Unemployment, now, had become a device of economic management and control. The problem, according to the government, was a vicious spiral of wage claims, leading to higher public spending, pushing up inflation. The government and the popular press thus found it easy to blame the trade union movement as a whole for excessive public spending, inflation, and rising unemployment; problems which actually had their roots in Britain's imperial past. This has set the tone of the years of the Thatcher government, with its fatalistic acceptance of mass unemployment and its hostility to the welfare state.

Important for this discussion of PEL is another set of ideas which gained currency at the time: namely, that poor economic performance was directly related to the poor quality of education and training. Comprehensive schools came under attack for having seriously undermined standards and neglected the most talented students. When James Callaghan opened the 'Great Debate' on education in a speech at Ruskin College, Oxford, in October 1976 (the same autumn that the first 'Second Chance to Learn' students enrolled in Liverpool), he was at pains to reject the elitism of the right. At the same time he argued that schools had fallen out of step with the needs of the economy. This line was spelt out still more explicitly by the Department of Education and Science (DES) Green Paper, 'Education in schools', when it asserted that one of the main aims of education should be: 'to help children to appreciate how the nation earns its standard of living and properly to esteem the essential role of industry and commerce in this process'.[3] The Great Debate is now largely forgotten,[4] but we are left with the notion that the problems of the economy and working-class underachievement can simultaneously be tackled by providing a stronger dose of technical and vocational education in the academic wastelands.

In chapter 3, I shall discuss in more detail the impact of these attitudes on the world of adult training. In Britain the tradition which separates education (a broad preparation for life and work with an emphasis on individual development) from training (above all focusing on job-training) has also kept separate the funding and control of these two worlds. In the mid-1970s, with a steady rise in unemployment and a consequent reduction in those jobs for which any training could claim to prepare, these distinctions began to look, to a lot of people, increasingly inappropriate. From 600,000 in 1974, the unemployment figures rose to a peak of nearly 1.5 million in 1977 (by 1985 reaching 3 million). Clearly, what was required was a thorough review of the entire field of education and training to take account of the new features of economic decline and rising unemployment. The objectives should have been to increase investment in human resources and to attack educational inequalities. Instead, we witnessed the sluggish response of education, whilst the Manpower Services Commission (MSC) set up in 1973 was confined to piecemeal experiments with retraining and schemes to recycle youth and adult unemployment. It would take the Conservatives to furnish a strategy that would tie education and training firmly to their view of how to organize the economy and the labour market.

Time off for training: the prevailing imbalance

Margaret Bird and John Killeen's report on PEL in England and Wales was not published until 1981.[5] Their survey, however, the only one of its kind so far, was being researched in the same year (1976/7) which I have taken as the starting point for this chapter. Sponsored by the National Institute for Adult Education, they worked full time for a year, with a staff of four and twenty-two sparetime voluntary research associates based in polytechnics and universities, to try to establish the extent and distribution of paid educational leave throughout the country. Most workers, they reported, received no paid release at all. Women, black people and the unskilled, being in jobs for which no pre- or in-service training had ever been envisaged, were least likely ever to have had any opportunities for paid leave. Training at work, traditionally, has been offered to skilled workers to become more skilled, as well as to technicians, managers, professionals and academics.

Based on an area survey of twenty-three local education authorities and a national sample survey of employing establishments, their research revealed that in 1976/7 between three and four million of these people received some sort of PEL (15–20 per cent of the employed population at the time). They add an interesting and, to us writing this book, a significant comment to their observations:

> The formal courses of instruction identified by our surveys, attended by employees released from the task with pay, do not exhaust all education with pay. *Paid education is integral to many occupations, particularly professional ones, so that deliberate*

> *release for specific courses does not apply*. . . . Conferences, study groups, seminars, working parties, the viewing of relevant films and so forth, are largely confined to those in managerial, scientific and professional occupations. Correspondingly, it is people in those occupations who are liable to enjoy conditions of service which, *contractually or by common consent and understanding, include paid time for self-improvement* and (sometimes) a degree of autonomy as to how and when it shall be used, so that the concept of 'paid release for course attendance' is inappropriate. [my italics][6]

Quantifying the exact amount of PEL at any given time, then, is no simple matter. And those of us who have put this book together have made no attempt to up-date the comprehensive researches of Killeen and Bird. All we can say is that, since their investigation, some small changes have begun to happen in the pattern of PEL. Low-paid and unwaged workers, white women, black people, older adults, in one or two places, have begun to wrest some time for their own development from the responsibilities they routinely carry out.

Of the PEL researched by Killeen and Bird, 99 per cent was for 'vocational' or job-related purposes. The only significant quantity of PEL that had broader purposes than this was that granted for trade-union education. The Health and Safety at Work Act of 1974 and the Employment Protection Act of 1975 both made explicit provision for union representatives to have time off from their usual work for training courses approved by, and state funded through, the TUC. As they point out, however, the gains conferred by this legislation were set within a context of 'collective bargaining to determine how the right to paid release will be applied in particular locations'. In our discussion about broadening the scope of PEL we must be aware of the limits to what legislation alone can achieve in bringing about a 'right' of this kind. The numbers attending regional TUC day-release courses certainly rose through the 1970s to a peak of nearly 44,000 by 1979, but the importance of such release for the union membership at large, let alone for all working people, was not to feature on the agenda either of the TUC or the Labour government during 1974–9.

For anyone without qualifications, either unwaged or employed, the chance to develop their own education or gain qualifications, as an adult, therefore continued to depend on their determination to do it in their own time, out of their own pocket. Adult education in the mid-1970s was struggling to respond to that kind of need, with intense debates as to what kind of provision would meet the needs of unemployed people, with the growth of 'Fresh Start' and access courses, and with an increased attention to basic education. The Callaghan government's public spending cuts, however, were soon to attack these beginnings, too. After 1979, under the Conservatives, a still more discriminating pattern began to emerge. Defence, law and order, and social security (to pay for the growing numbers of people unemployed or on low pay) were the chief beneficiaries; housing, health and education the main losers. Adult education, the main gateway for working-class adults, already with a mere 1 per cent of education spending, did not escape the axe. Fees went up, pressure to increase quantity of attendance at the expense of quality of learning grew, and funds to staff vital outreach programmes diminished. The result, reported in 1982, was an evident decrease in enrolment by working-class women and men in adult education classes.[7] Universities, of course, have suffered too, but the pattern of inequality, if anything, has been increased, with manual workers in 1984 still only occupying 20 per cent of places in higher education.[8] Seven years after Killeen and Bird's study, the same pattern of training opportunities still prevailed, the 1984 Labour Force Survey finding that unskilled jobs usually performed by women and black people were still untouched by any training programmes, and that only 3 per cent of any employees aged between 50 and 64 were being offered any training at work.[9]

In short, over the ten years 1976–86, there has been little change in the overall picture of lack of education and training for women and men who do not already possess qualifications.[10] Meanwhile, as full-time employment chances decreased, the number of part-time jobs have multiplied, rising between 1971 and 1983 by nearly 1.5 million – almost entirely accounted for by women employees.[11] As chapter 2 points out (see p. 29), for women in these jobs (concentrated in cleaning, catering, hairdressing, clerical and shop work) the prospects until recently for any PEL have been nil. It is a workforce about which the national training institutions are silent; yet their numbers are bound to grow.[12] Relying on the threat of job-loss, firms are forcing more workers to accept part-time, casual labour, frequently with a loss of benefits, and certainly with no intention of an in-service training programme.

Alliances and glimmers of hope

It's a gloomy picture. Yet in the same period, a whole range of creative activity persisted in pushing through; among others, some of the efforts described in this book. While the trade union movement, for example, was under persistent attack, with a fall in membership and a rise in employers' confidence, a number of unions developed important new approaches to education, precisely in order to rally an informed membership to the issue of the political levy (see p. 65). At local levels, the energy generated by collective campaigning for improved childcare, housing, and against racism, fuelled all kinds of self-help groups who then voiced claims on educational and other kinds of resources to continue their work. Trevor Carter, in his book *Shattering Illusions*, has shown how black organizations took the lead in combating the myths of black *and* white working-class educational underachievement, moving, in time, to a demand for more resources and control.[13] The movement of working-class writing and community publishing (which, also in 1976, first came together as a federation) originally consisted of a number of groups which, like Queenspark in Brighton, or Lifetimes in Manchester, had gathered together to campaign on local issues, discovering, in the process, the power of their own experience and the possibilities of themselves as writers and publishers of that experience. Some of them convened as adult education groups with a convenor paid as a tutor of the Workers' Educational Association (WEA). Others successfully obtained grants from arts bodies to publish collections of their writing. By 1980 over 120 such titles were in print and circulation. As their second anthology of writing indicates, this movement represented a growth in cultural activity intimately bound up in community action.[14]

It is no coincidence that the PEL courses we describe as existing models from which to develop a broader programme all include the invitation to their participants to develop as writers. All the chapters in Part II refer to the stress given in the courses on writing. Those classified as manual workers, whether waged or unwaged, have often, otherwise, had no other opportunity to shed the conviction that they are educational failures. The delight in finding out that they have things to say on paper which others could read, and the pleasure in being able to give mutual support and safely exchange constructive criticism is, for many, like a door opening after years of being shut in. Some 'Fresh Start' and literacy courses developed the practice of publishing magazines written and edited by students. It is at this point – in their sense of the power of words – that the women's movement and working-class adult education have converged, giving rise to a new school of literature, to which the Take Ten and Second Chance women's courses in Liverpool and

Southampton have all contributed. Feminism has made its mark on training, too (see p. 47); and the practice of the women's movement has had implications for a number of improvements to men's as well as women's education and training.[15] In literacy work as in women's studies courses, the stress on a collective, non-competitive style of work is fundamental, with teaching materials drawn where appropriate from the students. 'Workbase', the basic skills project sponsored by the South East Region of the TUC, is a PEL version of that practice (see pp. 94–107). For students who see themselves on the margins of both the employer's and the trade union movement's activities, this approach can offer not only a dramatic move forward in personal self-confidence, but also a kind of membership education.

First published in England in 1972, the work of the Brazilian educationalist Paulo Freire gave considerable inspiration to the growth, in the seventies, of a more radical approach to adult education. Second Chance, like other courses of the time, aspired to re-create educational opportunities which would be, in Freire's words: 'the practice of freedom, the means by which men and women deal critically and creatively with reality and discover how to participate in the transformation of the world'.[16] The course still describes itself, more than a decade later, as being 'for working-class adults who are concerned about the problems facing Merseyside'. Like other courses, both mixed and women-only, which took off soon after with similar titles and purposes, it discriminates in favour of the unqualified, or those who some call 'the disadvantaged'. These are courses which expect at least a working use of literacy, but which also ensure support in study skills and tutorials to enable unpractised writers to pursue the coursework.

Second Chance's declared aim to harness education to the needs and struggles of the working class collectively brings it close to trade-union education – and also to the '150 Hours' scheme in Italy (see chapter 10). This, too, rose out of the same period of extra-parliamentary struggle in the late 1960s and early 1970s. There is another important parallel. From the beginning, in 1973, the Italian trade unions, who negotiated 150 hours paid release for their members, welcomed the contribution of what was called the 'people's school movement' – a community campaign to reform the middle school in favour of the working class. This had two major consequences: first, from the start, the right of the unwaged to enrol for the '150 Hours' courses was established; secondly, '150 Hours' was able to draw on a revolution in techniques in adult education.[17]

So, for different historical reasons, but like Second Chance, '150 Hours' courses include adults both unemployed and employed and, of the employed, both those on paid release and those without this.

Within the trade union movement itself, suffering from the impact of mass unemployment and hostile legislation, there has been, it is true, a decline in WEA/TUC day-release courses, from 725 in the academic year 1978–9 to 319 in 1984–5.[18] Trade-union membership, too, has fallen back to the level it attained in 1972, but with a predominantly older age group. There has been a contraction in manufacturing and an expansion in local government, the health service, finance and banking.[19] With these changes, however, have come new kinds of activity. The Electrical, Electronic, Telecommunications and Plumbing Union (EEPTU), for example, has set up its own technical training centre to enable its members to acquire the skills demanded by new technology. The National Union of Public Employees (NUPE), with a membership dominated by low-paid workers, by women and by part-timers, as well as having many black worker members and members whose first language is not English, took a lead in responding to the needs of those workers. It was NUPE which negotiated the original agreement for PEL for London University domestic staff which led to the creation in 1978 of Workbase. It commissioned SCAT (Services to Community Action and Tenants) to produce publicity material for its members about privatization in the Health Service, and it has made considerable use of the Northern College ('the Ruskin of the north') for its courses. Other unions have experienced similar pressures to re-think their educational policy and, in particular, to find new ways of involving a broader cross-section of the membership in their day-to-day affairs. The result has been several new initiatives by the TUC in the fields of education for women, for the membership, and for unemployed people. Although the movement in general has been laggardly in putting its anti-racist and anti-sexist rhetoric into practice, several unions, including NALGO (the National Association of Local Government Officers) and ASTMS (the Association of Scientific, Technical and Managerial Staffs), now have separate courses for women and for black members.

As employers, the Labour-controlled local authorities have made a start in setting up equal opportunities training for their employees, in work time, without loss of pay. As chapter 8 indicates, Sheffield Council politicians originally saw Take Ten in instrumental terms, as a means of creating an ambassadorial force of council employees who would present the authority's view of its conflict with the

Conservative government. That vision was changed with the experience of the course; Take Ten is now understood to be a means of political education for those workers who, in the past, had been so badly served by education and training. It is also an attempt to install democracy from the bottom up.[20] Similar motives have contributed to the growth of other council-run training programmes, whether modelled on the GLC work of the early 1980s or on Sheffield's initiative.

Finally

At the time of writing (winter 1986), some two thousand people have taken part in Second Chance, Take Ten and Workbase programmes since 1976. This is a small beginning, compared to the one million who, since 1973, have attended Italy's '150 Hours' courses. Across the country, a sprinkling of other employers have also, over the same period, been persuaded to grant PEL to their manual and other low-paid workers for purposes of general education. It has been beyond our scope in this book to research all of these. They certainly do not add up to a systematic, planned strategy for release. As the incomes of the low paid and claimants are further eroded, their ability to meet even the fares to get to courses – let alone the cost of childcare, fees and basic materials – also falls. It is certainly no easier, in the mid-1980s, for working-class women and men to claim time for their own study and training than it was ten years earlier, the point at which this chapter began.

In spite of the small number of PEL courses we describe, their impact seems to be growing. Frowned on or ignored by central government and the Manpower Services Commission, uncertainly funded, and not fully accepted by the trade unions or employers – not to mention those in the private sector – their existence is always in doubt, and their capacity to move beyond the pioneer or experimental phase is still weak. Despite this, especially since 1979, PEL is not just being talked about more, but it is also being realized, at least in the public sector. Margaret Thatcher's re-election in 1983 put an end to the hopes of new legislation, however half-hearted, raised by Labour Party policy. The incipient debate between the proponents of a Minimum Educational Grant for All (MEGA) and a trade-union-led extension of PEL subsided. Other avenues have been explored instead. One of the most fruitful of these leads to the crossroads between political and basic education, and between trade-union education and employee training. The ambiguities explored in the four case studies in this book will not appeal to those who prefer to take their training or their trade-union education neat, but there is little doubt that, at least for the time being, schemes such as Workbase and Take Ten offer the best and most exciting means of extending access to those who would otherwise be excluded from post-secondary education.

2

Now or never: women, time and education

Jane Mace

Women and release: how much does it cost?

Few women's lives separate easily into 'work' and 'leisure'; and few stop working when they leave their 'workplace'. To divide up a woman's work into paid and unpaid may be important to her purse: but if we want to understand the importance of 'paid leave' as a means for low-paid and unwaged women to gain access to education and training, it's not a very adequate exercise. Black and white women have been saying for some time, of course, that such a separation won't do as a way of describing women's work; but it takes time for these things to be heard.[1] Fitting courses into lives already overcrowded with housework, childcare work, family work – 'other people work', in short – is not easy. It means negotiating (or fighting) for release from both paid and unpaid work; and for women to claim leave for their own education there is always a price to pay. Historically, working-class women have had to pay it themselves. In this book we argue that the time is long overdue for it to be paid, for once, not by women themselves, but by their employers and the state. PEL for women, then, both transcends economistic arguments and is intimately bound up in them. It cannot be done on the cheap, and it has profound implications for traditional assumptions both as to who is seen to be worthy of 'training' and what the purposes of that training is seen to be.

One cost is essential in the PEL calculation, and particularly for women if they are to be fully released from paid or unpaid work in order to pursue their own education. This is the cost of 'cover', or payment for another person to take over the woman's usual responsibilities. 'Cover' recognizes a woman as important enough to require replacement in her absence – whether from the job at work, or the care of others at home. In practice, there are a number of ways in which employers perceive 'cover': ranging from one worker doing part of another's job as well as their own, without any reward, to a properly paid full replacement. When 'full replacement' is not on offer for absences due to sickness or maternity leave, it can seem futile to suggest that a union should negotiate for it to 'cover' absences due to a luxury like education. (As one shop steward said to me: 'There's no point; we're already short-staffed, we get no cover when women are off sick, and management is talking of redundancies anyway.') Yet only with full replacement – having someone paid to do her job while she's away – can a woman fully regard herself as 'on leave'. For low-paid women workers, there are two almost contradictory reasons why this is so. Firstly, women in low-paid jobs are already in insecure and low-status employment. If a woman allows herself to go on a course in worktime knowing that her job is *not* being covered, she also knows that she is offering her employer the opportunity to make the old excuse for cuts: 'We managed without you'. She looks dangerously dispensable. Secondly, and in contrast to this, the more low-paid the job, the more noticeable to others can be the absence of the worker. Complaints about work not done are always more freely available to the cleaner or the clerical worker than appreciation of the everyday work that *is* done. Without 'cover', women such as those described later, who attend a course at work, simply work harder, come to work earlier, do their usual work faster. While anyone working for PEL courses must be acutely aware of the issue of cover (which is also one crucial to male low-paid workers), none of the PEL examples we describe in this book have fully resolved it – bound up, as it is, with recognition for the worker in the first place. (It's a problem which is, of course, common to trade-union courses for safety representatives and shop stewards as well.) Cover for unpaid work I'll come back to at the end of this chapter.

Employers with a declared commitment to 'equal opportunities' have some interest in demonstrating that they are implementing them. PEL for women manual workers is obviously a step in the right direction; but by definition, such course experiences will stimulate the women who take part to expect and demand other changes, even to dare to ask for still more leave for education. The danger of employers conceding short, one-off courses without other structural changes (such as reforming their procedures for recruiting, appointing and promoting staff, or developing a planned programme of training) is that these can simply feel like 'education-for-further-frustration'.

Nevertheless, PEL opportunities of the kind that courses like Take Ten in Sheffield can supply, even though the context in which they take place may not yet be ideal, means good news for low-paid women workers. Both in mixed or women-only settings they can, for once, enjoy the pleasure of rediscovering that they are already people with abilities, knowledge and skill. This sense of having worth and importance can be of enormous significance to those women who are most invisible to others: nightworkers, early-morning workers, servicing workers. What they have to say has an audience; and having the chance to write and be read within the course group has repercussions beyond the course itself. So while it is true that short courses of this kind are limited, and should be just one stage in a whole series of opportunities for low-paid women workers, it is also true that the personal and collective strength which they can develop has positive and immediate effects.

Both these problems and benefits were raised, for me, early in 1986 when I met with seven women in Sheffield to ask them how they looked back on their experience of attending Take Ten courses (see chapter 8 for a fuller account of these). Each woman spoke passionately about the delight of the course she had attended, and of the importance to her of it being timetabled within the hours for which she was paid. Each, too, in different ways, voiced the sense of disappointment later, when she tried to pursue, via further part-time or full-time courses, the appetite she had gained for education and training. As Kathleen, who had worked for seven years as a home help when her Take Ten course began, told me:

> This course gives you an idea of improving yourself, but in practice you just cannot do it...I've done a bit of nursing, clerical work, cleaning in offices, anything, you know. I'll try anything. But I do find it annoying that you're getting into your middle years and you could, you've got ability to do other things, but you don't have a chance.

Women, particularly if they are in their 'middle years', without a linear progression of full-time employment, are bottom of the league for in-service training. The excitement and pleasure of the short course that Kathleen and by now several hundred other women council workers in Sheffield and elsewhere have experienced has meant an important move forward.

As an employee of local government, Daisy, with others, learned on the course more about how the council worked than she had ever had the time, energy, or chance to do in the years she had worked for it. ('What I know now, I didn't know it four years ago', she said; 'and it's just because of the will to push it.') One thing she practised on the course was how to *use* these structures. Other workers had elected her to represent them as someone who knew how to speak up. What she learned during the course was a way to ensure that she was listened to: 'I always put my finger up and wait, because I was taught that way', she told me. 'They say, "All right, it's Daisy's turn now", and then I'll have my say.' I asked her: 'You were taught that from way back?' and she said, 'No, from Take Ten. . . . You have to keep on putting your finger, like you're bidding something, and then I make my voice heard.' As a black woman, she didn't need telling how white people, particularly in positions of authority, could make her invisible. What the course supplied was the chance to draw on that experience and practise a means to challenge it – through exercises, project work and discussion.

Timetabling time off

Chandana, at the time I spoke with her, was working as a childcare assistant. 'I have to tell you the truth', she said; 'I enjoy it, but I don't want to be a childcare assistant for the rest of my life, oh no thank you very much.' Of all the women I met, Chandana was the one with the strongest sense of a course in worktime being a means to move on to other work. For her, it gave her, most of all, 'more encouragement really, to do more courses' – something which had not been offered to her before. It had simply not occurred to the head of the nursery where she worked that a low-grade worker such as she should 'need' (let alone 'want') such opportunities:

> I'm not saying she was bad, because she was not; but she didn't realize that there is a need for people like childcare assistants or nursery nurses to go for training courses; she just thought that this is for teachers. It's a completely middle-class attitude, isn't it?

Like Daisy and Kathleen, Chandana obtained leave from her job to go on the course. She, like Daisy, is a full-time worker. Her two children, being very young, still claimed much of her time at home; and she had gained particularly important support from her union, NALGO, in gaining the maternity pay to which she was entitled at the time of her second pregnancy, a time when, with her husband unemployed, that money was of critical importance to the family economy. Attending the Take Ten course some two years later gave her the opportunity to pool this experience with others and gain a fuller understanding of herself as a trades unionist:

> While I was doing this course, the Take Ten, I became aware of certain laws and regulations of the union, and once you know all about it, well at least a little about it, it makes life easier, then you know where you stand.

A linguist in three other Indian languages besides Bengali, Chandana had previously worked as an adult education tutor of 'English as a second language' (ESL). There, the hierarchy of senior manager to worker is made more acute by the prevailing practice of employing hourly-paid part-timers, on fixed-term contracts, with no long-term benefits or security – and certainly no common practice of release on a paid basis for inservice training. While a majority of these part-timers are women, the decision-making power for curriculum and policy remains largely in the hands of men.[2] As to their own training and development, it must simply be 'fitted in' in their 'own time'. Chandana, who described herself as 'very strongly motivated' was, at the time I met her, going to an evening course in order to qualify for the Certificate for Proficiency in English: 'It's from seven till nine. So, coming back from school, making the tea ready and then going to the class – I sometimes do feel very tired.[1]

At a meeting of five of the women, a month after our interviews, to discuss what they had told me, Lucy, a library assistant (quoted in the introduction to this book), spoke of the gap between an employer's 'policy' and middle-management attitudes:

> I don't care what they say about policy-making, and what you're entitled to according to the town hall – it all boils down to your immediate superior. I mean, they're just so patronizing! 'I'd like to go on a course.' 'Mmm, yes, dear.' You know. 'What would you like to do?'. . . It's all right sitting here and preening ourselves, we all thinking we're wonderful in what we've done. When you actually get out in the outside world, people are still not interested.

Daisy had worked nights as a care assistant in a residential old people's home for six years when I met her. For night-shift workers, attending any adult education course, let alone one of that length (60 hours in 10 weeks) without relief from full-time employment, is hard, if not a serious health hazard. She knew precisely the importance of paid educational leave. Only the release from her Tuesday-night shift had made attendance at the daytime Take Ten course on Wednesdays possible for her. After this course was over, she applied to go on a Health and Safety course (one full day a week for thirteen weeks) for which, of course, the rights already exist to obtain 'leave'. It was refused her. Daisy tried to attend this course, this time, without time off work, leaving her job in the morning, after a night's work, to go straight to the college. After three weeks of this, she collapsed at college and was taken home in someone's car.

It was not, at one level, that Daisy's work was too little recognized or seen to be unimportant, that prevented permission being granted for her to have release for this second course. Rather, the attitude of her supervisor was, on the surface at least, that she was too essential. With just two staff on duty at night, and forty-four residents, Daisy's particular experience and skills were certainly invaluable. So the 'nuisance factor' of an essential worker being absent added to her supervisor's sense that the purpose of the absence was less than essential. What happened next is an interesting example of the devices that employers can use to block workers' claims for this kind of leave, while maintaining a position of apparent support for them. Having abandoned the effort of persuading her supervisor to grant the release, Daisy joined a Wednesday-morning English class at the local college. Soon after this, she was told that she could now have the leave she had asked for to attend the Health and Safety course – also on Wednesdays. Daisy explained that now that she was enrolled, in her own time, for the Wednesday-morning English class, she would have to go on the Health and Safety course that would run on Tuesdays, rather than the Wednesday for which she had originally asked.

> She said to me, 'Oh no, you cannot get the day on Tuesday.' so I said, 'Well, it's only common sense; the council already, management already grant me a day – so a day is a day'. . . So she said, 'No, you cannot have Tuesday, you have to have Wednesday.'

Daisy, in her 'own time' was committed to developing the confidence she had gained on Take Ten in her writing. She wanted leave from her nightwork on Monday night, rather than Tuesday night, to give her sufficient energy to attend the Tuesday Health and Safety course. It was that shift of timetabling which her employer was refusing. The retiming had all to be Daisy's, but, as she said: 'You've got to get time from work to learn. Anything you're doing, you've got to get time, and you've got to get paid.'

Women and unions: insisting on a hearing

Like many other part-time, women manual workers, Sheila had had little reason to feel part of a union. She had never, in the two years she had worked as a school-dinner supervisor, been to a union meeting. Her husband worked shifts; she bore the main responsibility of childcare for their two children (one of whom had been diagnosed with a rare disease in infancy); union meetings always took place in the evenings. The Take Ten course she attended was in the daytime, within her usual working hours. She recalled her reaction to the publicity leaflet for the course, when she first saw it at work. 'I'm the inquisitive type and I've always felt as though I wanted to do something else; I've never been satisfied with what I've got. So I wrote off', she told me.

It was, Sheila said, a mark of her increased sense of confidence, gained on the course, that she initiated, some weeks after it had ended, a piece of union solidarity at the school where she worked. The teachers' industrial action in 1985/6 in protest at government cuts in education obviously affected manual workers. On the day she recalled, at her school, with no cover by teachers for the dinner hour, the children were being sent home. The kitchen staff used the time to clean the kitchen premises. The dinner supervisors had no children to supervise. The head, that day, was off sick. The deputy head told her and the others that they would either have to get just half pay, or, if they came in, that they would have to 'scrub tables and wash walls down and things like that' with the kitchen staff, which, as Sheila said, 'is not our job'. She told me:

> With being on this course I got the initiative to go to the union and sort it out. . . I thought, 'I'm not losing pay' – I mean, why should I? But they (the other supervisors) all said they weren't going in. They accepted half a day's pay and did nothing. But I was going in, and do the full pay.

Sheila went to the town hall and saw the union official, who confirmed her hunch that their union had made an agreement on full pay for the supervisors – and that the deputy head was out of order in suggesting otherwise. Just to be sure, she also rang one of the other women who had been on the Take Ten course with her, whose husband, she knew, was a NUPE shop steward. He confirmed what she had been told. Having thus double-checked her case, Sheila said, 'I collected up all the other ladies and we all went in.' She told the head, who was back at work by this time, what had happened. 'It was only with myself going down that it got sorted out', she concluded. (The shop steward, she explained, worked in the kitchens, and 'didn't want to know...I mean, they were working all right, you see; she wasn't bothered about us'.) After the ten weekly meetings with other women workers which the Take Ten course had provided, the value of 'collecting together' had gained new meaning for Sheila. Clearly, it had also refuelled her determination to insist, for once, on being recognized and listened to.

Trade union procedures, like trade union 'business', have often overridden and ignored the specific experience asserted by black and Asian women, many of whom, over the years, have channelled their anger and frustration into other community and political organizations, into the growing welfare and social activities grown out of church membership, and into their own, autonomous groups.[3] Amrit Wilson, in her account of the 1976–8 Grunwick dispute, when Asian women were challenging not just their own exploitative employer but also the TUC, asserts that these strikers, who fought so long with such strength, 'effectively exposed once and for all the myth of the TUC's solidarity with exploited workers, and in the process of doing so...redefined the methods and outlook of industrial struggle.'[4] It would be hard to quantify how many other black and Asian women took inspiration from those in Willesden. At least in Coventry, from a study carried out by Barbro Hoel, it would seem that the decision by women in two Coventry clothing factories to strike against long-term exploitation took off in direct response to the determination and courage of the Grunwick workers.[5]

For Daisy there were no illusions about racism, in the union or anywhere else, when she accepted nomination as a NUPE shop steward. 'Waitressing and caring for the elderly' was how she summed up her considerable work experience to me when we met in her sitting-room in May 1986. It was precisely her capacity to 'survive', learned, as a black woman, 'the hard way', which led to her being offered, and accepting, the position of union representative. She told me how the other workers turned to her, following the frustrations and anger created at work by the behaviour of a newly appointed manager:

> Most of the staff is beginning to...some is leaving, and it's all aggro round the toilet corner, it's all aggro on the top floor, it's all aggro, you know, in the little corners, and it's break time and is all angry – but they won't tell her, you see. So there's all aggro, people spilling their guts out when she's not around...So he says, 'Go on Daisy, be a shop steward, we haven't got one here'

> because they know I can take up for myself and they know I can talk; I learned to survive, because you've got to learn to survive, and I learned the hard way...So I says, 'Well look, no one is going to walk upon me; you can do so much, but then I'm going to say, look, that's enough; enough is enough, you see.' So they says, 'Go on, go on, represent us' – and that's it. I said, 'All right then, I'll get a form.' So I've written off to the union for a form, and they sent me a form...and they fill it up, and there was 50 in there.

This, in itself, was the start of a new kind of work for Daisy; paperwork, evening meetings, 'every morning three or four letters coming through the door, telling you all things'. The opportunity to join the mixed Take Ten course with some dozen other women and men in the autumn of 1984 was the chance to take stock of her new role; as she told me, at that time, 'I didn't have my foot down yet as shop steward'. With two children grown up and college-educated, her own further education, in terms of organized study with others, had just begun.

Part-time work, part-time chances

While the number of full-time jobs in the last fifteen years has dropped, more and more women have had to take the growing number of part-time, low-paid jobs. By 1980, two out of every five women in employment was a part-time worker.[6] By 1984, 90 per cent of part-time jobs were being done by women (nearly 4 million). Part-time work, of course, as well as meaning low-paid and low-status jobs with exclusion from bonus schemes, sick pay, holiday pay and overtime payment, also means, usually, little or no access to training and little or no opportunity for promotion. To make matters worse, measures proposed in a government White Paper of May 1986, 'Building business...not barriers', propose to raise the number of hours of work per week (and continuity of employment) necessary to qualify for full employment rights.[7] Unions and campaign groups have been quick to point out the effect this has on women workers. Not least among the purposes of PEL courses timetabled within women part-time workers' employed time is that of ensuring that those women themselves are aware both of such rights as they do have and of the effect proposed changes such as these could make on them.

Many have more than one part-time job. Some combine a home-working job with part-time shifts outside the home. Plainly, part-time workers, already often excluded from other employment rights, have least chance of being granted time off for study. Black women, and those for whom English is not a first language, are particularly excluded from the world of training or education at work. Beverley Bryan, Stella Dadzie and Suzanne Scafe, who have documented the experience of black women's lives in Britain, describe how the lack of nursery provision has driven black women particularly to resort to homework, nightwork, shiftwork and part-time work in order to bring in a meagre wage. The pattern of everyday pressure which this implies brings its own toll of ill-health:

> For the working-class Black woman, it is true that avoiding high levels of daily stress is virtually impossible. The economic and social pressures of our class are acute because capitalism itself is in crisis, and we bear the brunt of that reality.[8]

In a study of 'stresses at work', Nicholas McDonald and Mel Doyle argue that the only way for the damaged health and social relationships caused by low pay, incentive payment systems, shift-work and other factors to be repaired is by 'workers having more say in the control of their working environment'.[9] For women employed to service that environment – cleaners – the stress factor, given the 'fitting in' of paid and unpaid work that has to be done, can be great. The space and time that a PEL course can offer is one certain means by which they can begin to have 'more say'.

It is hard for a woman paid to hoover a carpeted classroom to see that it is legitimate, in paid time, to be sitting down and 'studying' in it. Yet in-service training, conferences and the like, for those who teach in those rooms are regarded as essential to their work – regarded, in fact, as 'work' itself. It is one thing for her to have time out from cleaning in order to learn how to be better at the task of making rooms clean (and there are enlightened employers who, when the sales representatives of industrial cleaning equipment firms offer demonstration sessions, have been known to invite cleaners themselves to join them); it is quite another for her to be allowed to sit down, be listened to and, to a limited extent, serviced, herself. For while courses at work for low-paid women should, undoubtedly, be seen as serious work (as Mary Wolfe argues in chapter 7), it is also important that the women themselves experience them as *pleasurable* work; the kind that is recognized; the kind that affirms women not only in their role as 'workers' but as people with imaginations, visions, pain and knowledge too. This, certainly, is how courses in the equal opportunities training programme of the Greater London Council were presented and approached from 1982 until its abolition in 1986. Their aims, in the very first course run as part of this programme – 'basic skills' for part-time cleaners – were 'to give people confidence and independence', because they recognized that 'it is vital to people's personal esteem and self-satisfaction to be able to feel in control of their everyday life, at work and at home'. In one particularly practical sense this policy was given meaning. The GLC, as their report *Training for Change*, put it, recognized that cleaners, by the very nature of their work, would be especially 'aware of the standard of accommodation': 'An important factor, therefore, was seen to be the provision of proper training rooms and facilities in the Staff Training Centre.'[10]

In the autumn of 1984, a group of ten women staff attended a course in their working hours at Goldsmiths' College, London. Two mornings a week for ten weeks they sat down in a carpeted classroom instead of doing their usual work. All ten were employed by the college where they were meeting – the eight as part-time cleaners (two white, six black), the other two (both white, one of them me) as teachers. I had never worked in a job that started at 5.30 a.m., and this was the first adult education course I had taught that began at 7.00 a.m. All the 'students' in that particular class had already been at work an hour, doing a 'flick round' of the departments they were usually responsible for. At that time of day, the other college staff and students (including, usually, myself) – those whom these women 'service' with their work, every day – were not yet in the building; the committee members who met in the rooms they cleaned, to decide what academic work those rooms would be used for, were at home, perhaps just getting out of bed.

For this, the first course at work for those employees, management had approved their release – but not their 'cover' in terms of 'full replacement'. One result was that for most of the twenty course sessions, including that morning, at least two of the workers arrived up to an hour late in the classroom; another was that three of the original twelve dropped out altogether, not because they were ill or absent from work, but precisely because, with no 'cover', and other staff absences, they themselves felt unable to leave their usual work. Nina, who usually cleaned the college library with three others, had to drop out of most of the course, because one of her colleagues was off sick for some weeks and another was on maternity leave. For all the women, the lack of 'cover' for their own leave as for these more familiar situations was a frustration throughout the course. Their solution was that of conscientious professionals with high standards: to get in earlier and to work harder. Some increase in the migraines, backache and other symptoms of stress and ill-health from which several of them suffered already was simply an inevitable side-effect. Yet we worked together, touching on a wide range of subjects, reading other writers, interviewing each other, reading a play, discussing ideas about education, work, religion, politics, examining maps, translating statistics, discussing news coverage, writing letters, poems and stories and, all the time, working at and playing with language. For a small group of women who barely have the time to greet each other most other mornings in the year, and leave to go on to other responsibilities when the rest of us are just getting to work, it was an unusual experience. None of them had been to an adult education course like it before. Some of them, after it was over, joined a Fresh Start course in their own time. In 1986 I did too; as teacher for a similar course for women cleaning staff in Lewisham Council, once again, in their working hours, once again, in the early dark winter mornings.[11]

Women and maps

Yvonne Collymore was one of the 48 women tutors (in a total of 51) employed by the GLC to teach on their 'positive action courses' between 1982 and 1986.[12] When I met her in June 1986, she was continuing to work as a free-lance tutor of equal opportunities training courses in a number of London boroughs, in between running her own publishing business, 'Arawidi'. We discussed how women workers can be invited to see themselves as whole people, not just as 'the cleaner' or 'the clerical assistant'. As a teacher, and a black woman conscious of her own development and training, she felt it was important that her own experience could be drawn upon in the effort to persuade other women to re-examine their own:

> We often used ourselves as examples and talked about our career development [she told me]; and then gave them an exercise which helped them to map theirs out. And similarly with discrimination. We would give examples of discrimination we'd experienced and then get them to look around at that idea; and then we would get a whole range from the whole group. Which convinced the people who thought that there wasn't any discrimination, because they'd

> been all right, that there was quite a lot around. There were always a few.

Such as approach, in her experience, gives women workers (black and white, lesbian and heterosexual, old and young, disabled and able-bodied) 'one, the confidence that they're not alone; and then, the courage to actually work together, and use other people as allies to move, where they're going'. It's the kind of approach that literacy teachers have found useful, too (see chapter 6) – of which Yvonne herself (as founder member of the Caribbean Communications Project, in London) had experience. 'They're all job-related', she said, of the courses she taught:

> but we didn't ever have them completely and totally geared to just jobs.... I feel quite strongly that you can't separate your work from your life in two boxes without there being some interplay between the two. Very very few people can do it. So you actually need to look at yourself as a whole person.... In assertion training, it's geared to both work and home needs; because if you're not assertive at home, you may think you're assertive at work – but unassertiveness in any area affects your overall personality and confidence.

Nearly twenty years after qualifying as a teacher, and with considerable experience of training others, Yvonne enrolled on a thirteen-week MSC business course. This experience, as she said herself, led her to re-examine her own and other women's lack of a 'planned career':

> It was the first course where I actually had any time to focus on my own skills and my own future. I mean, I had gone to learn business skills: but it was very much a personal-development-based course, the way it was...geared to how the business was going to fit in your life and your needs; and where in fact were you going in your life, in five years' time. A question which I couldn't answer!...Most women don't have planned careers; especially women in our age group. We were encouraged to find something to do until we got married.... You weren't encouraged to see work as a long-term thing.

After she completed the course Yvonne was invited to teach on what was the first black-only course sponsored by the Manpower Services Commission, in 1982; and from there began teaching the 'First steps to management for women' courses run by the GLC. These, as she saw them, were able to 'break some of the myths about what management is about' for women:

> It's about giving confidence to women, first of all that they have skills, even though they may not have qualifications in the formal sense; and that over the years they have developed skills, either in running a home, or in doing voluntary work outside the home, or in their current job. It's usually a combination of all three. And we try to get them to look at their skills as broadly as they can; and they're usually surprised to find how highly skilled they are. We also do with them a bit of career planning. OK, you say you want promotion; where's that promotion leading you to, what do you ultimately want? They actually haven't thought that through. It's this five years' time thing.

This approach posed a direct challenge to a woman who until then had felt forced to acquiesce to her own subordination. It was exciting; and it was disturbing. Working at that time for the GLC, an employer with a declared commitment to radical reform of its own employment practices, such a woman had some chance of acting on this challenge, and having her new, more assertive identity recognized by promotion. 'First steps to management for women' were three day courses: two days, and then, some weeks later, a follow-up day. Yvonne Collymore recalled:

> Very rarely did we hold a follow-up day where there weren't at least three people who had got promotion out of the twelve.... Usually there was a pattern where three people got promotion, three to four people got interviews, and others had taken some steps to get into college, or whatever. But they had all moved.

Heady days. For most women in most jobs, the reality will remain rather less hopeful for some time to come.

The worm turns

This chapter has focused almost entirely on PEL for workers employed by local government (as do chapters 7 and 8). The few hundred women that these represent, who have enjoyed a first brief opportunity to study in their paid working hours are, of course, a tiny handful of the large mass of others, still being paid only 74 per cent of male wages and still largely concentrated in 'servicing' work.[13] For these, the interests of employers and profits remain dominant over theirs.[14] Certainly, while we argue (as we do in this book) for an entitlement to paid leave from paid work for women to take up their own desire for development, we cannot forget that, in present conditions, such an entitlement is not an easy one for women to embrace. Reactions from co-workers, not to mention those at home, are not always favourable to a woman's interest in her own education – let alone her development as a writer.[15] Janet, another Take Ten graduate and a part-time school cleaner, expressed something of this tension:

> I think it's drummed into you that you're a woman; you've been to school, you're a mother, and that's as much as you are. It's probably just a social stigma that sticks to you, and you don't feel you've a right to be anything else. And I must admit there were one or two of us that did say it made you feel very unsatisfied with your life, going there; it made you realize that I am a person, and I have got a right to say what I think, no matter who it's to. When I finished, I thought, 'Well, I hope that this confidence sticks to me.'

In July 1985, 8 black and 18 white women (whose ages ranged from 20 to 70) attended a four-day residential course at Hillcroft Women's College in Surbiton, Surrey.[16] None of the women there were on paid leave from employment – in fact, only 3 of the total of 26 students had full-time jobs, and another 4 had part-time work. Yet to get away from all the other people and problems for whom they were responsible required, for many of them, a major effort of will. (Between us, 30 in all, including the tutors, we shared responsibilities for some 48 children of varying ages.) However, the two essentials, in this pilot, 'linked learning' course, were there: every woman's accommodation was paid for, and special grants (childcare allowances) were available to pay for the 'cover' of their absence as childcarers. A lot of writing grew out of the talk that went on that week, using the themes of study chosen for the course: the four elements of earth, air, fire and water. Out of a conversation between seven students and two tutors on the last day, we made a poem, using the subject 'earth'. Without planning it, but rooted in the context of that week, the result reads as a metaphor for women's capacity to research and rediscover a collective power through companionable learning.

Earthworms
Digging into our minds

turning it over
excavating
  ridding the dry dead leaves
  and rubbish
Planting the seeds of ideas
pulling out old roots
preparing the soil
putting in compost
  running the soil through our fingers
  fertility
We are worms
wriggling in our confinement
dodging the blackbird
mulching
and airing
the soil.[17]

Nourished for once by other caterers and teachers than themselves, the authors of that poem, for a short time, were released for their own growth. The course in which it was written was not, as I've said, strictly a PEL one: only seven of the twenty-six women would usually have been employed in waged labour that week, and all of those were using their 'holiday leave' to be there. All had attended part-time courses in 'their own' time. The residential week had been aimed at those women who had taken part in Fresh Start courses in the London area. None of them, even with the payment both for 'cover' and other costs being supplied, had found it easy to negotiate the time off to come on the course (and other women, who had applied, had had to drop out at the last minute, because of those difficulties). All of them, once there, had a commitment to use the time on the course to its fullest. The sense of such time being a wicked treat, which every woman had to justify to herself (not to mention to her possibly less than delighted household on her return) may have contributed to this. The women there needed to believe they were working, not just enjoying a break.

3
Why training matters

Martin Yarnit

A lot of money is spent on training. Estimates vary, but it probably takes at least 45 per cent of the total spent by government and employers on adult education and training, including further and higher education.[1] Had this book been published five or ten years ago, I suspect that this chapter might have been missing. So what has turned training into a question of more than specialist concern? Why does it matter? And is there a coherent alternative to the strategy developed by the Manpower Services Commission (MSC) on behalf of the Thatcher government?

Too important to leave to the state

Training, or work-related education, mobilizes enormous resources primarily for the sake of national economic efficiency and, more specifically, to benefit individual employers. The rising arc of concern about the use of those resources coincides with the sharpening decline of the British economy since the 1960s and, above all, the return of mass unemployment in the mid-1970s. Since 1979 there has been a government with a clear idea of the purposes of training and with the determination to implement it. Its agent has been the MSC, a body whose capacity to intervene in the labour market is without precedent in peacetime. The scale and rapidity of the changes it has wrought have weakened and confused its opponents, whether in the trade unions or the education establishment, or amongst workers.

However, it would be a mistake to pretend that the problem with training began with Mrs Thatcher's election in May 1979. Training has always been geared to the needs of employers rather than the interests of employees; and it has always neglected the interests of most employees. Only a minority traditionally receive any preparation for employment, whether it is called education or training. Paid release, the chief means by which individuals find access to training if they are employed, is organized in such a way as to keep most people out. As John Killeen and Margaret Bird's study showed, paid release is largely the preserve of managers, technicians and professionals, the majority of them male and white.[2] They found that most release was granted for employer-run courses. Only 20 per cent of those on paid release attended at a college. Of these: 90 per cent were aged under 30 (their study excluded under-19s); 16 per cent were women (although women comprise over 40 per cent of the employed); and 50 per cent were managers, professional or technical staff (who make up 15 per cent of the employed). Unskilled, semi-skilled workers, part-time and shift workers, older workers, black workers and white women workers all received very little PEL at all – other than those on TUC courses. In gross terms, there is no reason to doubt that that is still the situation a decade later.[3]

It is not merely that the whole structure of educational finance conspires against those who miss out in the race for university entrance or other advanced courses. There is also the deep gulf (see p. 12) between education and training. The terms themselves convey less a distinction of aims than a notion of breadth and narrowness, a polarity that is reflected in the university–polytechnic dualism that crowns the British educational system. To put it another way, education provides transferrable skills; training is often not merely job-specific but employer-bound as well, especially at the lower end of the occupational hierarchy.[4] In short, whilst education implies a benefit to the individual as much if not more than to the economy or employers, training tends to reflect the needs of the employer above all.

Put this way, you might expect the trade unions to have put training fairly high on their list of priorities. That is certainly the case for the craft and technical unions, which have long been used to exercising substantial control over apprentice training. It is also true that the TUC was keen to see the MSC set up, at first to reduce the anarchy of the labour market and, more recently, to offset the effects of unemployment.[5] However, the trade union movement has found great difficulty in evolving a policy towards the millions excluded from training provision. Shop stewards' committees often have a Health and Safety representative, but very few have a member with responsibility for training. In part, this reflects an understandable political ambivalence. Trade unions have had a direct interest in controlling the apprenticeship system as a means of managing supply and demand in the labour market. Beyond that, training is often seen as a threat, as a tactic for reinforcing employer control dressed up as technological progress. The result is that the trade unions have paid scant attention to training as a mechanism for contesting managerial control over the work process. To a degree, that challenge has been mounted through trade-union education, but it is worth recalling Killeen and Bird's finding that only '29,000 of the estimated one million people to obtain PEL provided outside the employing establishment did so in their capacity as trade unionists'.[6] If the trade unions have generally failed to contest the aims, content and distribution of training, it is hardly surprising if the individual worker fails to do so. Traditionally, therefore, training has been seen in Britain as primarily for the employer's benefit.

A growing body of opinion finds this unacceptable. The rise of unemployment has sharpened the black and feminist critique of structural discrimination; and precisely because of the shortage of jobs, more importance is attached to the opportunities opened up by training (not that qualifications provide an automatic guarantee of access to either employment or promotion). The MSC is under growing pressure to provide equal opportunities on Youth Training Schemes, and many other public and private employers are at least compelled to outlaw discrimination in their public pronouncements.[7] Practical changes, however, are slow in coming in the mainstream training institutions. (Meanwhile, a lot of energy, as we shall see later, has been flowing into the creation of a substantial body of alternative schemes, often funded by local authorities and the European Social Fund, rather than by the MSC.)

Training in decline

Opening up training opportunities for workers and for unemployed people was one of the prime purposes of the MSC when it was created in 1973, which explains the committed support it has always enjoyed from the TUC. Training Opportunities (TOPS) courses were aimed at people who wanted to break out of their limitations and acquire new skills. They were also designed as a way of bringing unemployed people back into the jobs market. The preparatory courses which, from 1975, provided such an important opening for those with basic education needs, represented a bridge to the TOPS courses – at least in the first couple of years from their creation. (The importance, and eventual dismantling, of these courses is discussed in more detail in chapter 6.) The MSC refused to accept responsibility for the childcare provision on these courses, but it did pay a training allowance; and of all its adult training initiatives, TOPS has probably been the most warmly applauded by students and its critics. The courses certainly varied in quality, and the Skillcentres have never fully adapted to the needs of black people or white women. Perhaps significantly, the MSC quotes figures for black and women entrants to TOPS courses, but not completions. Nonetheless, 35 per cent of TOPS entrants in 1984–5 were women, 18 per cent from ethnic minority groups. Many if not most of these were unemployed, unqualified or low paid; exactly the kinds of people with whom this book is most concerned.[8] The early growth of TOPS was dramatic, from 29,000 places in 1973 to 94,000 in 1977, and then the numbers began to fall. Only 75,400 people completed in 1984–5, even though, judging by the enormous rise in unemployment alone, there was clearly a case for expansion.[9]

TOPS' fate is not isolated; it reflects a decline in the importance of training in the eyes of the government and the MSC, as a detailed examination of the Commission's budget demonstrates. The table showing MSC expenditure from 1981/2–1984/5 is abridged from their *1984–85 Annual Report*. The central point to note is that the Youth Training Scheme (YTS) and the Community Programme (CP) account for about two-thirds of total spending for 1985, an absolute and relative increase over 1981/2. Nearly all the other major spending categories are in decline:

1 Job centres down from £145m. to £130.6m. (these are all cash prices; adjusted for inflation the decline is far steeper).
2 Industry Training Organizations down from £117.4m. to £17m.
3 TOPS 'up' from £235.1m. to £235.2m. This represents a drop in real terms of 27 per cent.

Sheltered employment is one exception to the rule.

On the other hand, there are two new growth areas:

1 Enterprise Allowances, rising from zero to £80.1m.
2 TVEI, the Technical and Vocational Education Initiative, which has grown from £7.2m. to £26.6m. in the space of one year.

Counting TVEI as part of the training division, for the sake of argument, the proportion of the total budget going to training was:

1981/2	1982/3	1983/4	1984/5
67.57%	64.9%	59.3%	56%

MSC expenditure 1981/2 – 1984/5, cash prices, £ million

	1981/2	*1982/3*	*1983/4*	*1984/5*
Employment division	161.1	168.7	192.6	240.2
Professional and executive recruitment	5.5	4.3	−0.1	−0.1
Training division*	751.0	868.4	1,042.3	1,136.7
Skillcentre training Agency				4.9
TVEI			7.2	26.6
Support services	27.4	28.8	30.3	29.9
MSC spending on behalf of Dept of Employment**	166.5	267.2	496.6	637.4
Total	1,111.5	1,337.4	1,768.9	2,075.6

MSC *1984–85 Annual Report*, 37.
*includes YTS and TOPS
**includes Community Programme

Thus, on the MSC's own definition of training, its investment is in constant decline, from over two-thirds of total spending at the beginning of the decade to, if the trend persists, one half by the late 1980s.

What does this change mean? Firstly, it reflects the government's preoccupation with the unemployment figures. The response to the spiral of adult unemployment was at first sluggish, but between the financial years 1982–3 and 1983–4, spending on CP more or less doubled in real terms. Secondly, whether because of budgetary pressures or political preferences, training has come to be seen less and less by the authorities as the leading edge of the MSC's labour market strategy. Skillcentres have been forced to become self-financing on pain of closure. TOPS is in rapid decline and its important full-time training allowances all but gone. Apprentice entry is at a historic low and the Industry Training Boards reduced from 23 to 6. Some training, with MSC encouragement, has been picked up by individual employers, rather exceptionally as Sir Keith Joseph recently observed, or franchised to private training companies, which have mushroomed of late.[10] However, most that passes for training, in the MSC's definition, is encompassed by the Youth Training Scheme: a scheme which, despite the best endeavours of some training agencies, is as much about reducing the unemployment figures and conditioning school-leavers to flexible, low-paid work as about qualifying for employment.

The roots of the problem

Training's decline pre-dates Mrs Thatcher's election in 1979. Arguably, it never enjoyed a heyday, but it did at least experience an upturn in the sixties. The 1964 Industrial Training Act was an attempt to make a break with the past and to put vocational education on a rational footing. With the limited exceptions of some big public and private enterprises – ICI, the Civil Service, British Rail – British employers have waged a protracted campaign against any legal obligation for training. Small firms would argue that they couldn't afford to train properly, whilst bigger companies resented the loss of trained workers poached by unscrupulous competitors. With concern growing amongst politicians and economists about Britain's declining position in world markets, industrial training clearly could not be left to the whims of individual employers.

The 1964 Act empowered industry training boards (ITBs) to levy employers and to disburse money to pay for college and company schemes. However, it was never fully accepted by employers and a continued rearguard action, concerted by the Confederation of British Industry (CBI), led in 1973 to a generous exemption scheme. As Maureen Woodhall points out: 'In 1977–78, the potential income from the levy amounted to £200m, but the actual levies received were reduced through exemption to only £81m.'[11]

The pre-Thatcher industrial training board system had other glaring defects. It covered less than 40 per cent of the workforce and even then was oriented almost exclusively to craft and technical workers. Thus, whilst skilled manual workers accounted for about 45 per cent of all the training, only 2 per cent of the participants were women.[12] Although more recently some ITBs developed a concern for equal opportunities, the post-1964 training scheme retained a traditional conception of vocational education to the exclusion of a broader vision of the value of personal development. There were exceptions. The Local Government Training Board has moved from a strict concern with skill transfer to understanding the importance of public service; but this is far from the mainstream of training.

Under Conservative control, the MSC swiftly abolished sixteen of the training boards and returned the others to direct industry control. In cash terms, its grant to the boards fell from £117.4m. in 1981/2 to £17m. in 1984/5, almost a ten-fold reduction in real terms.[13] Devolving training to individual companies is more than a cost-cutting exercise. It reflects the idea that private enterprise knows what is best for it, should be relieved of the burden of state bureaucracy and will produce the training that best suits its needs. It was precisely the failure of this approach which led to the 1964 Act. Now, it is likely to narrow opportunities and course content. Employers will tend to make their training, if they mount it at all, job-specific, to fend off poaching by rivals. Market pressures will squeeze out social considerations, such as the need to open up training as engineering technicians to girls.[14]

The 1980 report on 'Education, training and industrial performance' deliberately looked at education from the 'limited perspective of the needs of the economy'.[15] Such a view was by no means novel, but it reflected the changing climate of thought after the so-called Great Debate of 1976 about education, initiated by James Callaghan and his Education Secretary, Shirley Williams (see p. 12). They wanted to see a shift in the aims and curriculum of secondary education to bring it closer into line with the needs of the economy. The underlying premise was that Britain, unlike its competitors, refused to take industry and trade seriously. The alternative view that the country's education and training structures were dangerously selective was overtaken by a new orthodoxy claiming that the good of the economy required schools and colleges to focus on employers' needs above all else. The Conservative policy built on this, using the MSC to transform not only training but also to edge into DES territory. It has won the right to control 25 per cent of non-advanced further education, and this, coupled with the financial pressure on Local Education Authorities, is impelling further education towards a more market-led view of its reason for being. In the secondary schools, TVEI is re-creating the old technical school – an implicit accusation that comprehensives have little to offer the majority outside the A-level streams. Training is bending education towards that same 'limited perspective of the needs of the economy'.

Filling the gaps

The history of training and education since the Great Debate demonstrates that a viable alternative to the employer-led, market-oriented policies of the MSC requires quite different starting points; but first, what are the present gaps in provision for adults? There are two ways of approaching this question. One would be to survey the market and pinpoint the demand – an enormous task, if done thoroughly. The evidence is that the demand for good training far exceeds the supply. (In its first year, South Glamorgan Women's Workshop (SGWW) had four times as many applicants as places.)[16] The alternative is to look at the kinds of people who get a poor deal from our present training institutions.

Women receive a small slice of the national training cake, largely because they are concentrated in the jobs and industries where training is poorly regarded by employers. Training, where there is any, tends to be rudimentary, on the job, and with very little time off for linked courses. Typically, whereas 34 per cent of men between the ages of 16 and 19 in employment receive day release, only 10 per cent of women do, mainly for hairdressing or office skills. Only 1 per cent of women trainees in 1981 were in engineering or metalworking.[17] This is not to say that all women's work is unskilled or does not require training, but rather that it is undervalued and that employers often rely on the informal transference of skill. This, however, can sometimes rebound on them, as Helen Rainbird's study of one company's approach to re-organization illustrates:

> In their haste to let people go, they lost skills which were essential to production. These skills, though not formally recognised, had been acquired through experience, and were based on knowledge of the system, the product and an ability to identify faults... Although the jobs were considered to be semi-skilled and requiring manual dexterity rather than diagnostic skills...the company had to bring back these unskilled women workers who had been made redundant...to train the new employees.[18]

Women who are unemployed may be so because the lack of childcare and other facilities (and assumptions by fathers) require them to be the primary carers of children, at the expense of any paid job they could take. They may be actively seeking work, even so – as, of course, are those women without such responsibilities. Many take low-paid shiftwork, part-time work, or home work to eke out low incomes. In all these situations, black and white working-class women who don't happen already to have qualifications (and many who do) face a variety of obstacles in achieving the training they want. Many are excluded from training, whether deliberately or not. Worst of all is women's exclusion from Skillcentres, with fewer than 3 per cent of places: a reflection, in part, of an exaggerated concentration on training for 'male' trades, such as building, motor mechanics, and engineering.[19] Not surprisingly, an MSC report on women in Skillcentres found that nearly half the women questioned believed such centres were for men only.[20]

The Community Programme (CP), despite its poor investment in training and its mostly part-time hours, can still be useful for women wanting a foothold in employment; but only 24 per cent of them get places on the scheme.[21] This is the result of the MSC's policy of barring married women who are not claiming unemployment benefit.

Women who are not even registered as unemployed – and taking them into account could almost double the national rate for women's unemployment – are even lower on the MSC's list of priorities. (Only claimants now count in the official unemployment figures.) TOPS courses, it is true, do offer women a better deal, although here they are down from 43 per cent of all trainees in 1980 to 35 per cent in 1984.[22]

Women who want to go back to employment after a period of domestic work, then, face both the reluctance of potential employers to recognize the value of their experience, and the expectation that they will find personal solutions to their childcare problems. Many are forced to accept low-paid, part-time jobs in which any qualifications or skills they possess are disregarded.[23]

Black people fare worse than even white working-class women. Pakistani and Bangladeshi women have the highest unemployment level, with four in every ten out of work. The official survey from which this statistic is taken notes that 'possessing a higher level of qualification did not appear to reduce unemployment rates for ethnic minority groups to the same extent as it did for whites'.[24] A Labour Research survey of race discrimination in local government found that black people were concentrated in the lowest grades, whether manual or non-manual, and that, despite equal opportunities policies, in only five of the twenty-six authorities which responded did the percentage of black workers employed exceed the 1981 census figures for black people living in the community but born outside the UK.[25] Taking into account that the actual number living in an area will be much higher, 'it is likely that, of the authorities surveyed, only Lambeth and Hackney employed black people in proportion to their residents'.[26]

Despite this, only 8 per cent of CP places go to black people;[27] and despite Section 37 of the Race Relations Act 1976, which allows positive discrimination in training, the MSC maintains that 'discrimination exists in society and in employment and YTS experience is reflecting that. . . . It would be wrong to look to training schemes of any kind to solve more widespread problems of discrimination in employment.'[28]

Alternative objectives, alternative schemes

Sheila Marsh, whilst head of the Greater London Training Board Support Unit, put forward a set of possible training aims: (1) serving economic efficiency; (2) serving public service provision; (3) serving political development for individuals or groups; (4) promoting equal opportunities and positive action to work to redress past discrimination; and (5) promoting social change – providing some of the means whereby society can move to a more equitable distribution of resources and power.[29] The value of her approach is that by counterposing to the needs of economic efficiency a set of aims that scarcely figure in most discussions of training it challenges the idea that the employer knows best. How well do these aims relate to what is happening? Are they a useful aid to understanding the objectives behind some of the new training initiatives on the fringes of the mainstream? In reviewing Sheila Marsh's categories, the only examples I have found have been promoted in the public sector. This is not because here, or anywhere else in this book, we wish to celebrate local government as the sole provider of good training; it is simply that initiatives of this kind, it seems, are not to be found in private industry. This underlines our central argument: that training, left to employers without public accountability, will remain an activity centred on their interests.

Serving economic efficiency Training for employment which tends, by definition, to aim at meeting the needs of employers can also benefit others. In Sheffield, two linked schemes are also about producing something of value to the community – houses. Sheffield Works Department has created a new apprenticeship training scheme on a new building site in the Manor area, following a precedent set by Hackney Direct Labour Organisation. The building scheme will include a training centre where half of the Department's apprentice intake will combine practical and theoretical work.[30] The Young Women's Plastering Project is a council-supported independent initiative aimed at opening up one building trade to women. The Project will help to ensure that the Manor scheme meets its equal opportunities commitments.

Serving public provision Involving low-paid, usually manual workers in publicizing their work and improving the service to the public in the face of threats of privatization has been the stimulus for projects such as the Women's Employment Project in Haringey, which has developed with school-meals workers' plans for extending their role into nutrition and children's play supervision, underpinned by an appropriate training package with an anti-racist, anti-sexist perspective.[31] In Bradford, similarly, a training scheme for school cleaners funded by the Equal Opportunities Commission (EOC) aims to open up opportunities for promotion to caretaker as well as producing a training pack for use by other local authorities.[32]

Political development for individuals and groups Bradford Council is increasingly coming to recognize that it needs to listen and respond to what people want, and therefore needs 'a workforce which is aware of the social repercussions of its work, which is politically more sensitive'.[33] In Sheffield's Community-Work Apprenticeship Scheme previously unemployed women and men undergo a three-year certificated training in youth and community work while working in a council department. The main aim is to open up council employment to local working-class people, particularly black people and women, which both helps to make a significant contribution to thinking on local accountability and develops the ideas of the apprentices themselves about the role of youth and community work and the problems of change in public service.

Equal opportunities and positive action For some people, this *is* the purpose of training. (Indeed, an equal opportunities strategy in training may have more success in changing the composition of a workforce, when linked to a similar approach to recruitment, than training for employment does in getting people into jobs.) A growing number of new schemes are for women or black people only, in some cases taught by an all-women or all-black staff on the basis of the neglect of training and employment opportunities for those groups. (Skills shortages as much as legal obstacles make some schemes more dependent on male or white tutors than they would wish.) For women with children, perhaps the most crucial aspect of any training scheme is whether it offers childcare; but as important as childcare to many women, according to the women's worker at Camden Training Centre, is the provision of English as a Second Language (ESL) courses. Camden and Haringey Women's Training and Education Centre (HWTEC) provide ESL with printing or pattern cutting or computing.

Promoting social change Although improving public services or taking positive action on training contributes to promoting social change, that is not the central objective. The difficulty in identifying a scheme which does prioritize social change as its objective suggests that this is a gap in provision that needs filling.

Where does all this leave us? Is there something here which amounts to a coherent alternative strategy for training? Schemes such as those outlined here show that there is some room for manoeuvre in asserting the needs both of the individual and of the collective, whether that means trade unionists, the users of a public service, or even the long-term interests of the working class as against the short-term economic concerns of employers. To put it more positively, the struggle against racism and sexism in training may be making a significant contribution to the growing self-confidence of black people and women in demanding employment and power. There are other cases one could draw on as well.

Two arguments could be put in reply. First, that the growing pressure for equal opportunities in training merely underlines the difficulty of making headway in employment. Second, that progress in mainstream provision is frustratingly slow. The answer is that it is still too early to tell. What is clear, though, is that even if the emerging alternative training system does make headway in challenging the MSC, the ITBs, and the other major providers, its main themes will be the need for fairness and equality rather than a radical overhaul of the economic system. A less inflexible society than Britain should be able to cope with more Blacks in technology industries, with a more broadly based form of work preparation, with more women managers, with training that helps workers to challenge the organization of production. Since the signs are that it cannot, the gently progressive nature of the new training initiatives may be mistaken for a revolutionary onslaught, and treated as such.

New initiatives in training

In short, there is no coherent alternative strategy. Instead, there is a variety of answers to the question, how to break the grip of the market on training. This ought not to be belittled. Market forces are currently very strong, given the policies pursued by the Conservatives since 1979, and it is important to show that these alternatives are possible, even if they are small scale and confined to the public sector. These can be divided into two groups: preparing for training, and training for employment.

PREPARING FOR TRAINING

There is no lack of demand for high quality training, but schemes are often concerned to target their recruitment at specific priority groups. Close links with the local community and its organizations are essential, at least at first, and that is why Camden Training Centre employs an outreach worker; although for South Glamorgan Women's Workship 'the significance of word of mouth has increased as the Workshop has become more established'.[34] Training schemes can also act to increase understanding about what is on offer by mounting bridging, introductory, or taster courses, as they are variously known. In Sheffield, for example, the polytechnic runs a residential course to introduce young women to engineering while they are still at school. Strathclyde has a similar introduction to science and technology.[35]

TRAINING FOR EMPLOYMENT

What ingredients make for a high success rate in placing trainees in jobs, the central aim of all training for employment schemes? The experience of Camden Training Centre, a limited company largely funded and controlled by the London Borough of Camden, suggests that two elements are crucial to its 78 per cent rate: the right courses and an integrated system of support for trainees. It has developed through experience a mix of courses which attract trainees and which provide skills needed locally, and an employment liaison worker acts as an intermediary between employers and the Centre, finding and monitoring suitable placements, and looking out for suitable vacancies. The Centre's annual report contains a two-page, closely typed list of the firms which have helped in some way. Intervention in the labour market, rather than desk-bound research, is the main way that the Centre maintains the link between its programme and local demand. Although its principal objective is to find jobs for trainees, it also takes seriously some of the other aims identified by Sheila Marsh, particularly the promotion of equal opportunities,[36] by means of a nursery, ESL courses, and an education support unit, of which the latter is the most unusual feature. The Centre, by arrangement with a local college, has a team on site which provides individual counselling, advice on money matters and educational opportunities, as well as course components on employees' rights and trade unionism – thus allowing it to tap into a network of education, training and employment resources.[37]

Sheffield and Leeds City Councils, too, have both been developing training since the early 1980s as part of their policies on employment and equal opportunities, but both have chosen to create or support individual projects rather than set up an integrated training centre. This arrangement has the disadvantage that information about the local employment market and even the local authorities' own education and training resources may be fragmented or duplicated. In addition, apart from the scale of the resources required to provide enough places, many training schemes of this kind are forced to cope with too many other dilemmas to be able to devote themselves single-mindedly to training for employment. Women's technology workshops, for example, are struggling to provide two years' training in one, and to hold on to their European Social Fund (ESF) funding at the same time. Some schemes are trying to juggle a set of mildly contradictory objectives: can we train for employment and encourage trainees to be critical of the anti-social uses of technology? Problems of this kind are hard to resolve in any conceivable society, but some of the others demand clear thinking and commitment in local and national government and in the trade unions.

Finally, of course, if training is a serious enterprise, it makes no sense to regard what happens to the trainees in their first jobs as incidental. The transition to employment requires active supervision and monitoring at close quarters. Many training schemes are so hard-pressed simply to maintain themselves that they have little energy left for follow-up work after training, but it is crucial. A lot of effort is invested in placing trainees in jobs, but supporting ex-trainees in the first six months of employment is vital. After the protected environment of many schemes, the real world of employment can be an unbearable shock with, among others, the major problem of finance. To maintain the relatively low standard of living that a training, travel and childcare allowance plus housing benefit brings requires a weekly take-home wage of around £130, far more than most ex-trainees can expect in their first job. Women paying for childcare, once again, are the worst hit. We live in a country which currently provides full-time nursery places for 20 per cent of three-year-olds compared with 88 per cent in France.[38]

National policy

Despite their difficulties and their scale, the training initiatives described here, on the edges of the state system, could well form the basis of a reorganization of vocational education, given certain changes in national policy. It is increasingly obvious that changes are urgently needed. The chairman of the MSC has conceded that the abolition of the ITBs and the training levy has not worked.[39] The National Institute for Economic and Social Research has drawn attention to the consequences of the contracting national training budget.[40] Training cannot be left to individual employers; even when they do it well, they fall down on quantity. It cannot even be entrusted to ITBs in a revived form. Black people, people with disabilities and unemployed people, women: a majority of the population will want to make sure that they will not be excluded from new training and paid release arrangements as they were in the past. *Nor can training continue to be exclusively about skills for the job*. Everyone needs to understand employment law and the role of the trade unions. We all need a better grasp of the educational and training opportunities now available. Accountability to the consumer, especially in the public sector, should impinge on training. However, there are limits to the extent that training can be wrested from its narrow concern with economic efficiency. For many, if not most workers, training will always display two shortcomings. Its narrowness will constrain them to their present employment, rather than opening alternative paths of career development; and it will be too concerned with the world of work. We must, it seems to me, address the relationship between education and training, occupying, till now, largely separate existences, to the benefit of the small élite. If we are serious about changing training, we can no longer afford to regard it in isolation. A daunting agenda follows from this statement. Here there is only room to touch on two points. First, we need to redress the balance of the last five to ten years. The influence of education should be extended to training, rather than the other way round. In particular, training should become less narrowly employment-orientated, and the training of unemployed people for employment should embrace a greater emphasis on personal and intellectual development. Second, education and training access and finance should be reorganized to provide broader opportunities at every level, without the intolerable burden on adult returners. It is unacceptable that the predominant model of university-level education, three- or four-year full-time courses, should be beyond the reach of people who cannot devote themselves to such an extent or who cannot afford to. What is needed is a network of education and training, with various points of access, flexible financial arrangements and co-ordinated information and advice. What we have is rigid, exclusive and incomprehensible.

4

Time off and trade union education

Peter Caldwell and Dave Eva

Today there are perhaps 300,000 shop stewards, including a number who are solely responsible for representing members on health and safety issues. (Safety representatives with legal powers were introduced in 1978.) Each year a sizeable minority pack it in, retire, leave their job or lose a contested election. In addition, work groups are persuaded for the first time to elect a steward and the union is recognized for the first time in additional workplaces. There could be anywhere between 20,000 and 50,000 new stewards every year.

Despite the devastating effects of de-industrialization and cuts in employment on the bargaining strength of employees, the shop steward remains the first line of defence for most employed trade union members. It is to the steward that people will turn when threatened with disciplinary action, when injured at work or when they have a grievance against management. The steward is approached and expected to 'sort it out' by providing the relevant information, meeting management or resolving a disagreement within the section. For issues which are beyond the scope of the steward to deal with directly, they remain the main source of information and the channel through which membership opinion is expressed to union policy-makers.

The provision of some means of encouraging, supporting and developing each new generation of stewards and activists is a major educational project, especially in today's wintry and – for trade union activity – uninviting climate. Working-class adults – and especially manual workers – are often extremely apprehensive about the educational process. Asked about their expectations, stewards often say they expected courses to be boring, passive and repetitive – rather like their experience of school, in fact. In addition, many have reservations about what they see as their own educational inadequacies, and difficulty with spelling, for example, can have a very powerful inhibiting effect. Another source of reservation is the union itself – will the education consist of flow-charts of union structure? Will it be full of jargon? over my head? irrelevant? too political?

Stewards enter education feeling they have a lot to learn, are willing to try but not convinced that it will work. PEL is crucial in tipping the balance and persuading potential students to get involved. The bulk of steward education nowadays is organized on a paid-release basis, usually consisting of: two or three consecutive days; a week's residential course in a hotel or union college; or one day a week for ten weeks. Much of the discussion in this chapter draws on the last (10 × 1 day) but experience on other courses is not dissimilar.

What does education offer the new steward? Essentially it provides the opportunity of time and space away from the pressures of work and home in which to reflect on the experience of being a steward and to discuss it with others. It is important that people can feel justified in taking this time; it's not stolen from domestic commitments, and the worker is entitled to take it away from usual work. The sharing of the experience with others is a strong point; courses often include a wide variety of people from different occupations, ages and unions (on TUC courses) as well as gender and race, linked together by the common bond of being recently elected stewards and a shared feeling that this is an important and worthwhile role. Uppermost in many new stewards' minds is the fact that that role requires them to deal with management.

At times in the past it has been common for management to give some measure of support to steward organization. The approach more recently has been to undermine them. Rather than using stewards to communicate with workers and seeing their role as a source of information, management will go to great lengths to undermine or by-pass the steward and communicate directly with members through videos, briefings and direct mailing to their homes. Increasingly, too, they will try to restrict the facilities available for stewards and attempt to reduce their numbers. More disturbingly, stewards can face harassment, victimization and even dismissal.

At the same time – in a defensive environment – stewards have to try to engage with a range of new and complex issues arising from the restructuring of work. New health service stewards may find themselves competing for their own jobs as services are put out to tender. Stewards in manufacturing are confronted with a battery of new management control techniques accompanying the introduction of new machinery and systems. Internal changes in the workplace have been accompanied by external ones, notably the introduction of new labour laws that restrict and threaten local union leaders.

Whilst new stewards may see their role mainly in terms of their immediate constituency and dealing with local (or first-line) management, they will also have to confront broader issues and to participate in some wider organization. Most new stewards will find this intimidating (unless special efforts are made to assist them); representatives of groups that have traditionally lived on the margins of union organization will find this doubly so. Night-shift and part-time workers may well find the local leadership is dominated by full-time workers on the day-shift. In white-collar unions, low-paid workers may find their union branch executive dominated by better-paid professionals. Having got to the meeting and plucked up courage to speak, such stewards may then find little interest in or understanding of their demands. Black workers, particularly, often find that local trade union leaderships do not take seriously their problems with discrimination and with deportations.[1]

This is not just a problem for those groups, but for the continuing vitality of the trade union movement. New potential activists and leaders can drop out quickly, and members can become disillusioned; yet it is precisely in those areas of part-time and scattered employment, with substantial numbers of women and black workers, that potential trade union membership is greatest. Meanwhile, for them to get together for even a brief meeting to discuss a common problem represents a political and logistical triumph.

Clearly, what has been in any circumstances a difficult role, is today extremely so. This underlines the necessity for new stewards to receive comprehensive support, encouragement and education. Much of this is (or should be) provided directly by the union and its workplace leadership, but education in a more structured and traditional sense does play a crucial role.

Learning to be effective at work

The way learning is organized will vary between different schemes, unions, tutors and student groups. However, the basic aims of such courses are well summarized by the TUC: 'The course helps participants to develop the *confidence* and *skills* they need to be effective union representatives at the workplace.'[2] Learning methods have been refined to meet these aims. Here are a few common features.

Often courses are organized in the form of *course meetings* for all or part of the day. Students elect a chair, who convenes the day's meeting and chairs the discussion, and a secretary who takes notes and prepares a record of the day's work (minutes) for the following week. The course provides an opportunity to develop and practise skills, such as convening meetings, leading discussions, taking notes and summarizing arguments, which are used off the course. This way of organizing a course is often more accessible to trade union students and therefore more successful in bringing out their experiences and commitment.

A great deal of emphasis is placed on *learning and doing*. Students are encouraged to take initiatives at work, and in their unions, and to report these back to the course, discussing and analysing them with their fellow students. Where possible, case studies and problem-solving activities are drawn from the experiences of the students on the course: 'We've covered a few of the things that have been bugging me for some time', said Jenny, a National and Local Government Officers Association steward representing members in twenty different clinics,

> and a fortnight ago we did a marvellous experience. We used this one particular clinic which I know is overcrowded. There is also, from a health and safety point of view...poor lighting...a toilet that leads directly from an office where there are six people working – and we had a really good debate about that.... Mark [the tutor] made us work and find out all the facts for ourselves. And we split into three groups; we had the management, the unions, and an observer group, and fortunately I was on the union side and won![3]

The course Jenny was on contained a good *mixture* of people: a health visitor, a contingent from the local bus depot, several factory workers and a teacher. Nearly all found this mixture beneficial:

> One of the main things I've learnt is that although we're all working in different places...we all had very similar problems. And listening to other people, how they've dealt with things, of course some of them are much more union minded than NALGO. It's really been beneficial to me.

The opportunity provided by union education to meet stewards from different backgrounds is one of its greatest strengths, and a means to combat the isolation experienced by so many trade unionists. The practice provides the experience of a supportive collective environment. It encourages students to take initiatives, gain in confidence and skills, and in so doing change their relationships outside the course with their members, their shop stewards' committees, or their union branches.

The interaction between the learning process on the course and development outside it is brought out in this conversation between Derek (a steward) and a WEA researcher. Derek is the only steward in a sheltered workshop for the disabled where the union has only recently been established.

Derek: When I first came here I was expecting to, like sit behind a desk, listening to someone just waffling on and I'd be just yawning my head off all day. But the way it's run it does make you more active, it makes you want to take part in actual fact. . . so it does give you the confidence as well.

Researcher: What do you mean by confidence? Can you define it?

Derek: Well, I was always a bit shy and reticent about speaking in public. I mean, I admit it, I still am, but not as much as I used to be; I mean now, I go into the management, I say, 'Look, I want this doing' (it's either a safety hazard or it's against the health of the workers). 'Could you do something about it?' I'll go in, just knock on the door now, whereas before, I'd really have to think about it, try to work my courage up to go in. Now, it just doesn't bother me.

Researcher: Why does the course help you do that?

Derek: I think it's making us work as a team. You split up into groups and you, like, you're looking at one part of the problem, while another group is looking at another part. Say one part plays the part of the union – the other plays the part of management. So if you're the union you say, 'Look, we've got to do this', and someone says, 'Where can we get this information?' So we split up into that little group and say, 'Let's get this information from here, from here, who's going to be secretary and take notes? Who's going to be the speaker?' So we are working as a team, and I think that is helping me go back to my workplace, go back to my members and say, 'Can I count on your support when I go into management?' And they say 'Yes'. And when I've got the confidence of the workforce behind me, that gives me much more confidence, say, to react to the management.

Researcher: Is it the way you learn as well as what you learn?
Derek: We set our own prospectus on what we want to learn in the way we want to learn them.

This conversation engages with the concept of *confidence* – the strongest theme to run through working-class adult education. In this case, it draws out the relationship between the stewards' confidence in themselves and their relationship with their constituencies, and, in turn, their effectiveness as stewards. As Derek comments:

> Before I came on this course they treated me as a toy shop steward. I didn't know anything, nothing was going to change. As this course has progressed and I've had some success, and I've not been frightened to call in the district official when required – by keeping them informed – they are coming to respect me as a shop steward.

The teaching of *skills* and *issues* is approached in such a way that people do things on the course that are relevant and useful off the course. Taking notes, or keeping a written record of meetings or events, can be a difficult habit to develop.

> My education from the past hasn't been that great, because I just went to a London school where they put you in and kicked you out – there was always an opportunity to go out to work whatever you wanted to do. So when I came to put things down on paper, my brain becomes very lazy. . .working in a factory.

This is Mike, a steward in a car factory, who left school twenty years ago in the boom time. Not surprisingly, he found it quite heavy going writing up the course minutes.

> I spent near on three hours trying to put these minutes together. I got them together fairly well in the end, but I found quite a problem doing it. There were lots of bits I'd liked to have put in but I tried to have it condensed down like everyone else from previous weeks had.

Once outside the course, however, this particular experience seems to have been worthwhile:

> I need to take a lot more notes because my memory isn't that good. I did come up against the situation with the foreman. . .I came back out of the office and I wrote everything down that the foreman had said to me and when I went back in the office with a member of the EC [a senior steward from his department] I

> quoted it all. His comment was, 'I see you've got it in joined up writing.' He was trying to throw me, for a kick-off. But it definitely worried him that I'd written everything down.

As Jenny, Derek and Mike have described, the learning of skills such as note taking, finding information, preparing a case, negotiating with management and speaking in public, are woven into the fabric of the course and connected to the stewards' own aims in the workplace. In the same way, issues are discussed which draw on the experiences and priorities of the students. Members of one course had asked to watch a film about Nissan, the Japanese car manufacturer, and had a long discussion about it afterwards. Reflecting on this later, Maggie (a steward in the Coventry plant of a transnational machine tool company) described how this had helped her to make sense of recent events: 'It was an eye opener; that's what these quality circles are, getting you in groups, talking to you, pushing the union out. I didn't see it at first; that is basically their idea.'[4] Brian, on the same course, came to similar conclusions;

> We've just had a very difficult period at Motor Panels with an outright attack on trade union organization...and Nissan's quoted all the time by the company. Our works director has been to Japan and come back with all sorts of fancy ideas and he's actually tried to implement one or two, like quality circles.... Initially, you chair it; they make the steward feel very important, you're at the hub of things...they go into it and over a period of time you go away from the situation where they're going to the steward. They go to the men direct.

On this course, stewards from three different workplaces had picked on an issue they wanted to discuss – that of changing management techniques. The process of comparing experiences and looking at Nissan had helped course members like Maggie and Brian to re-examine their own experience. For this to be possible, courses require resources, and students require time and freedom from external pressure. Alongside the students, the primary resource in union education is the tutor. TUC courses work on the principle that one tutor works consistently with a group of students. In single union courses team-teaching is common, a tutor working with a union official or senior representative. Tutoring stewards' courses is a demanding task, as well as an exhilarating one. Each group of students needs to be planned for individually. Sharing control with the students is an important principle; but getting democratic relationships to work in the early part of the course can be hard. However, where a course does begin to 'run itself', the tutor has more scope to work with individual members, to identify useful resources, and to make more strategic interventions in discussion.

In addition to the tutor, a successful course requires information resources, and the materials required for activities like making posters and leaflets and drafting and copying documents. Over the last ten years there has been an enormous improvement in the resourcing of union courses. The TUC provide impressively printed workbooks for their core courses and most unions issue course packs and folders. Videos are an increasingly common feature of many trade-union studies centres; and, in addition, there is a plethora of pamphlets, leaflets and posters produced by the TUC and unions as well as by supportive organizations such as the Labour Research Department, the Low Pay Unit, the Child Poverty Action Group and the Work Hazards Group.[5]

In recent years, the availability of time and freedom from pressure for trade union students to gain from the experience of education has been largely dependent on the evolution of a system of paid release, the growth of which I will now summarize.

The growth of trade union PEL in Britain

Trade union PEL in Britain has developed in a very patchy and uneven fashion. Since the 1920s, both the Workers' Educational Association (WEA) and the National Council of Labour Colleges (NCLC) provided courses for their union affiliates. Whilst the bulk of WEA courses were evening classes or weekend schools, the main offering of the NCLC was correspondence courses. In the post-war years, there was a growing trend for unions to sponsor their own educational programmes, often focusing on developing the skills of branch officers and other activists. The 1940s and 1950s saw the beginnings of union courses organized on the basis of paid release from work. The National Union of Mineworkers, notably in Yorkshire, Derbyshire and Nottinghamshire, put considerable resources into courses organized with some of the northern universities. These provided a thorough liberal adult education spread over three years for a group of workers who had usually left school at fourteen or fifteen with minimal qualifications.[6]

In the late 1950s, the Transport and General Workers' Union (TGWU) took the initiative in setting up courses for car workers' stewards in Birmingham and Coventry.[7] This period saw the slow growth of paid release courses in industrial relations for stewards mainly in the car and engineering industries and provided by local authority technical colleges or by the WEA. Often the initiative for these courses came from the growing cadre of industrial relations lecturers who used their links with local employers to convince them that releasing stewards for courses served the interests both of employers and unions. Part of this argument was constructed as follows:

> The kind of education now required by unions which can be supplied by technical colleges lies in what might be described as a politically neutral area, e.g. the study of techniques such as work study, i.e. cost control and the study of legislation and the constitutional functions of institutions in the industrial relations system.[8]

At this stage, there was a continuing growth of such provision and support for it from employers' organizations, as well as the willingness of some Industrial Training Boards to use their powers to refund to employers the costs of releasing stewards for courses.

In 1965, the TUC established its own regional education service, absorbing in the process the separate WEA and NCLC schemes. From the beginning, the TUC's policy was to promote the expansion of day-release courses for shop stewards. (For the time being they retained but did not expand weekend courses, which ceased in 1974, and correspondence courses, which persist but are now rarely used.) As far as the government was concerned, the TUC, in trying to expand shop-steward education, was pushing at an open door. From the mid-1960s, state policy was increasingly concerned with 'reforming' shop-steward organization and an expansion of training was seen, by Labour and Conservative governments, as a part of this process. Steward training featured in the Donovan Report,[9] in the *In Place of Strife* proposals[10] and was the subject of a major report by the Commission on Industrial Relations (CIR).[11] The Department of Education and Science (DES) encouraged this development – shop-steward training providing an important new market for the burgeoning business studies departments within further education. A DES report in 1973 envisaged considerable public sector educational resources being made available for this work.[12]

Whilst state, employers and unions were in a sense moving in the same direction, important areas of conflict and ambiguity remained to be resolved. The main features of TUC policy were as follows:

1 A *comprehensive* system of steward education should be established, providing opportunities for all stewards. This suggested a massive expansion; in 1971 the TUC estimated that the average

voluntary union office holder received less than one third of a day's training per year. A figure of 10 per cent turnover among 300,000 stewards indicated the need for 30,000 annual places for new stewards alone. The TUC established the target of a 30 per cent annual rate of increase in the number of places available.

2 Steward education should be *independent* from the employers. This was the most controversial aspect of TUC policy, as there was a strong body of opinion amongst employers, some unions and some educationalists, endorsed by the CIR report, that industrial relations training should be done jointly by unions and management. The TUC were rigid in their opposition to this. ('We claim the right to determine the training of trade union representatives on the achievement of trade union objectives. This is a principle from which we will not deviate.' Len Murray, 1975 TUC Congress.)
3 There should be a *balance* in provision between TUC and individual union courses. TUC policy recognized that some unions wanted to retain their own programmes and felt that there were some areas they preferred to control themselves.
4 Union education should be *publicly funded*. Money was an important underlying issue in policy debates. Union subscriptions in Britain are comparatively low and union leaders were unwilling to commit substantial resources to education. In any case, they pointed to the substantial public funds available for management training (in 1973, the TUC estimated that this amounted to £12–15m. a year compared with £0.5m. on union education) and to the willingness of governments in other countries, most spectacularly in Sweden, to allocate public money to union education.
5 Union representatives should have a *legal right* to paid release for training.[13]

In the event, the Labour government elected in 1974 accepted most of the points in TUC policy and, during the course of the 1974–9 government, introduced them as part of the *Social Contract* package. Beginning in 1976, small annual grants have been made by central government under existing regulations to help fund TUC and union courses, tutor training and course development work.[14] At the same time, Local Education Authorities allocated additional tutorial resources to TUC work. Then, in 1978, the Code of Practice on 'Time off for trade union duties and activities' came into operation. The latter, made under Sections 57 and 58 of the 1975 Employment Protection Act provided union representatives with the legal right to time off for training.[15] In October of the same year, safety representatives under the 1974 Health and Safety at Work Act gained the same right. This legislation restricted time-off rights to representatives, and specified that the training should relate to their role as workplace negotiators.At the same time it institutionalized the control of unions over training, through specifying their role in approving courses.

The implementation of the right is contingent upon trade union organization: unions are needed to exercise the right and to negotiate over the details such as how many stewards should attend which courses and when. In this way, it could be seen as encouraging, or underpinning union organization at the workplace rather than in any sense replacing it. Although representatives denied release have the right to complain to an industrial tribunal and claim for lost wages, the intention was that disagreements should be resolved through negotiation. The strong advice of the TUC, in their pamphlet *Paid Release for Union Training*, was that the legal right should be used as a spur for collective agreements on paid release (a model agreement was provided) rather than as an excuse for litigation.

Subsequent experience suggests that this approach to legislating for paid release has both strengths and weaknesses. Where workplace and district union leaders encouraged and facilitated it, take-up of the right to release was high and participation in union education programmes rose impressively. The number of courses run under the TUC scheme rose from 643 in 1973/4 to 3,100 in 1978/9.[16] Within this, the capacity of union education to respond to the creation of union safety representatives was especially striking. For stewards' committees willing and able to take advantage of what was available, it was possible for all new representatives to receive training within months of being elected and for others to receive follow-on and refresher courses. On the other hand, participation remained extremely patchy, despite this expansion. Groups that lacked the information, encouragement and bargaining capacity often remained outside, scarcely participating at all.

Participation in union education has also proved, not surprisingly, sensitive to shifts in the overall bargaining climate. Since 1979, participation has tailed off and certain trends are beginning to emerge. Whilst introductory courses for new stewards remain buoyant, follow-on and health and safety provision has shrunk noticeably. At the same time there has been a tendency for short (two- or three-day) courses to replace longer (ten-day) ones. In addition, dependence on state funding for much of the provision has given the government a pressure point to influence the shape of the provision. Despite the TUC's strong views on independence, a category of course has been introduced for which employer endorsement is required.[17] However, there is no evidence that this has been used to restrict trade union independence.

Experience with paid release for steward's courses suggests that there are a number of issues which merit discussion, especially in the light of any extension of paid release or attempts to expand working-class adult education. These issues can be summarized under the headings of access, curriculum and methods, and resources.

Access

Participation in these courses requires a stable union organization, acceptance by management of the stewards' legal rights and some measure of support and encouragement from local union leaderships. Local surveys suggest that participation is much stronger in larger manufacturing companies and the public sector (mainly local government and the national health service); and in practice, many groups are excluded even though they have the legal right to participate, notably in workplaces where the local union leadership is unenthusiastic or hostile to education or where the employer succeeds in persistently obstructing the right to release. It is common, for example, for release to be granted but no cover to be provided, leaving stewards to have to complete their work on their return or to have it covered by colleagues. Working or domestic patterns of many stewards may make participation difficult or impossible. A worker on the twilight shift, sharing childcare with a partner, would face great difficulty attending a course from 9.00 a.m. to 4.00 p.m. In practice, too, part-time workers tend to lose out even when their hours coincide. A part-time worker would generally get paid four hours (if she normally worked a four-hour shift) for attending a course lasting six hours, whilst a full-time worker would receive eight hours pay for the same six hours.

At a wider level, current arrangements exclude non-stewards, including those union members and activists who do not have recognition from their employer.

The need to take union education to a wider membership who are not entitled to paid release is becoming a major priority for union educationalists. A popular approach has been for unions to arrange for the TUC to train some of their more experienced stewards as *discussion leaders*, developing their ability and confidence to organize informal educational sessions at work – in tea breaks, at lunch or as part of workplace union meetings. General social contact and conversation between members is used to introduce slightly more structured discussion about issues of concern to them. The public employees union, NUPE, has gone to considerable lengths to support and encourage these initiatives, producing a regular education bulletin (giving tips, ideas and information to discussion leaders) and a range of accessible materials that can be used to inform workplace discussions. Materials cover many of the issues that form the subject of workplace discussion – cuts in public expenditure, women's rights and union legislation, for example. In addition, every opportunity is taken to talk about the benefits of union membership to new starters, students, Youth Training Scheme trainees, or people on Community Programme schemes.

Scattered employment and irregular hours mean that these strategies cannot be confined to working hours. The shop-workers' union, USDAW, have encouraged the growth of *study circles* – small groups of members meeting in each others' homes and working with learning materials supplied by their union.

A parallel approach, undertaken by the TUC and individual unions, has been to target particular groups and run courses specifically for them. Many unions run regional and national courses for women members and, in the West Midlands, the TUC co-operated with the Indian Workers' Association to run a mother-tongue course for Asian workers. Other courses have been arranged specifically for groups of part-time workers, such as bar-staff, at times and locations suitable to them. Thus, there is growing evidence of unions trying to broaden the appeal of their educational programmes and find ways of involving more people.[18] This good practice remains, however, on the margins. For it to be brought into the mainstream will require a combination of a wider entitlement to paid release, a vigorous 'take-up campaign' by local union leaders and tutors and a more varied range of educational programmes designed for different groups of members.

Curriculum and methods

Earlier in this chapter we described the approach to curriculum and methods developed by trade union tutors. It attempts to blend the building of confidence, the development of skills and engagement with the main issues facing students. Within the curriculum and course materials, *equal opportunities* (anti-sexism, anti-racism, support for the rights of workers with disabilities) and an emphasis on greater trade union unity, take a prominent role. Tutors are expected to raise these issues when students neglect to do so.

Most tutors feel that great progress has been made in developing a pedagogy that draws on the commitment and experience of the students and meets their aims as actual, or potential trade union activists. This is especially important given the success of steward education in attracting thousands of participants with no previous post-school experience and, indeed, strong misgivings about any form of structured education.

There have, however, been strident exchanges between tutors about the value of this approach.[19] The TUC programme in particular has been subject to sustained criticism for an over-emphasis within the curriculum on workplace issues and for the way in which experimental teaching methods (especially course committees) have been encouraged. These have, it has been argued, led to an over-dependence on students' experience and interests. These critics would like to see a much broader curriculum dealing with social, political and economic issues in a more sustained fashion. Their model would probably be the three-year courses for miners (see p. 59), along with some of the work undertaken by the WEA and the NCLC prior to the establishment of the TUC scheme. To what extent this could be established on a paid-release basis without very considerable union funding is open to question but, as the critics have shown, the existing fairly narrow release rights (for courses 'relevant to the industrial relations duties of the representative') fall short of the TUC's aims and restrict the scope of the curriculum.

However, in a more modest way, unions have been introducing more political themes into union education outside the framework of PEL and state funding. The spectacular success of the campaign to retain political funds (and to establish new funds in two cases) was in part attributable to a mass political education campaign. Workshops, briefings, discussions and publicity won over many members to the value of a levy to support political activity by their trade union. The campaign drew on many of the approaches developed in union education to engage thousands of members in discussion and activity. In the Tailor and Garment Workers' Union, for example, it brought a whole new layer of women members into activity in the union and undoubtedly contributed to the increased representation of women on their executive in the 1985 elections.[20] For many union members, especially those in the public sector, the borderline between workplace issues and political/economic ones is a fine one. Issues like privatization, cuts and deregulation have stimulated a mass of informal educational activity. As well as this, educational strategies have been used to raise and popularize issues usually seen as marginal to union activity. NALGO in the West Midlands produced a video as part of their campaign against the deportation of a NALGO member and this has been used extensively on educational programmes. Many unions have produced educational materials on issues like abortion, sexual harrassment, gay rights and antiracism.

The extension of the curriculum of trade union education can be approached in two ways:

1 by unions making greater use of educational activities to inform their campaigning and policy-making work. Education has demonstrated its value here already and its extension could transform participation in trade unionism;
2 by unions taking the lead in campaigning for and organizing educational opportunities for their members on the basis of paid leave. Obvious areas to start with are *basic education* and *second-chance* education. In Sweden, for example, trade union study circles cover subjects (such as language courses) that unions would not be involved in in Britain.[21]

Finally

There has been in the last decade a considerable investment of resources in union education, both from the public sector of education (perhaps 200–300 public sector tutors work full-time in trade union studies) and from unions themselves, mainly through the appointment of education staff at national and regional level. However, the sector remains, like most of adult education, extremely under-resourced in comparative and absolute terms.

There is no reason why it should be. The resources released by the falling school population are sufficient to fund a systematic programme of working-class adult education. Learning opportunities could be provided for the least qualified and skilled groups who have borne the brunt of the massive changes in the labour market. Unions, as the writers of chapters 11 and 12 argue, have a crucial role to play in campaigning for and delivering a system of education that is of a high quality and accountable to its students. The success of shop steward education demonstrates the strength of such a perspective.

5

Paid or unpaid workers? Unemployment and release

Liz Smith

Why should a book about PEL include a chapter on the unemployed, who, by definition, have no paid work to get leave from? The answer is a simple one. In a country where unemployment is high and increasingly long term, to look at education for paid workers alone is to consign the unemployed and unwaged to the margins of a service or activity that can, above all others, bring them back to the centre.

In this chapter I will argue that the changing nature of employment makes a clear distinction between employed and unemployed difficult to draw, and for this practical reason alone it is preferable to talk of a 'system of education' within which the similar and differing needs of all workers are met.

The Merseyside experience

For the last six years I have worked on Merseyside with key organizations concerned about and resisting unemployment. Merseyside was no stranger to mass unemployment when it became a national problem in the late 1970s and early 1980s. The closure of large and recently established factories – hailed in the 1960s as the answer to Merseyside's problems – signalled to trade unions and communities alike that the region was facing deep-rooted and long-term problems, unlikely to be solved by the fickle private sector.

In 1981 several significant events prepared the ground for an organized campaign against unemployment. The first People's March for Jobs took place, with marchers converging on London amidst publicity and considerable anti-government propaganda. The reception which the marchers received as they travelled through Britain suggested widespread disillusionment with government policies and a refusal to accept ever-increasing dole queues. The Merseyside contingent on the march was large, organized and planning how to continue the campaign for jobs back home. During the same year, the TUC passed a resolution at its annual conference calling on affiliated unions to retain, and where possible recruit, the unemployed into their ranks and to set up TUC unemployed centres within which the unemployed could organize as part of the trade union movement.

More locally, Merseyside County Labour Party included in its 1981 election manifesto a commitment to set up a trade union and community resource centre within the county. This proposal already had the support of Liverpool Trades Council, whose employment sub-committee had called for a base for the trade union and labour movement in Liverpool, where the campaign against unemployment could be effectively organized.

The largest union in the region – the Transport and General Workers' Union – grasped the nettle of unemployed membership when, following the closure of Standard Triumph and later Dunlops, the 6/612 General Workers' Branch continued as a branch for redundant workers and later recruited both unemployed and employed to its ranks.

In early 1981 a collection of people from trade unions, the Trades Councils and other groups came together to form a steering committee to set up a trade union and unemployed centre on Merseyside, registered with the TUC as an unemployed centre. Based firmly on established and progressive elements within the mainstream trade union movement, an organization grew with the real potential to put the slogan 'Unemployed and employed unite and fight' into practice.

In drawing up the terms of reference for its unemployed centres, the TUC placed education at the top of the agenda. On Merseyside, unemployed workers, if nominated by their unions, were able to attend the main TUC programme for shop stewards and to participate in a growing programme especially for unemployed workers. The model for education and organization of the unemployed was in the tradition of the trade union movement. Unemployed people, usually isolated from other individuals and organizations, had the same need for representation out of work as in. Unemployed centres aimed to educate, train and support unemployed activists who would publicize centres, recruit into membership, represent members at the DHSS and encourage involvement in the wider trade union campaign against unemployment.

Shop stewards' education equips trade unionists with the skills and confidence to represent and defend their members and to understand the social, political and economic context within which they operate. In the same way, education within unemployed centres focused, on the one hand, on skills of representation, publicity production, meeting procedures, etc. and, on the other, on an understanding of unemployment and the key social issues directly affecting unemployed people.

As well as a general unemployed activists' programme, courses were promoted which aimed at specific groups of the unemployed, notably at women, who face the same history of male domination within TUC centres as they do in trade union branches. Courses about health, and women's role in trade unions and history were part of a general attempt to involve women in TUC centres.

My role in the period 1981–6 was as a founder member of Merseyside Trade Union, Community and Unemployed Resource Centre (MTUCURC), and later as President and Vice-President of the organization. At the same time, because of my job, initially at Northern College (as a tutor organizer responsible for courses for Liverpool students), and later with the WEA (as tutor organizer for the unemployed), I promoted educational activity within TUC centres on Merseyside. As well as TUC courses on welfare rights, basic skills, equal opportunities, unemployment and trade unions, there were facilities provided by other groups at the Centre. A variety of organizations ran courses, for example, on new technology, video production, photography, music workshops, assertiveness, basic business skills, workers' co-operatives, current affairs, labour history, women's studies and citizen's rights.

All of these varied educational activities and the organizations that provided them were united by a shared support for the Centre's aims and objectives: to promote the interests of working people and their organizations, and to encourage links between the employed and the unemployed. Education in this framework had to be active, challenging, collective and ready to address the political problems of the day. On Merseyside, that meant unemployment, above all.

Three assumptions lie behind all this and must be substantiated: firstly, that the distinction between the employed and the unemployed is increasingly blurred; secondly, that the educational needs of the employed and the unemployed are not radically different; and, thirdly, that to bring the employed and unemployed together is desirable in itself.

It is generally agreed that the labour market is undergoing major changes which – even with a different government – will affect our working lives into the forseeable future. Whilst there is disagreement about the reasons for these changes, the move towards part-time, temporary and contract labour, with the parallel reduction in full-time permanent jobs is clear to economist and lay person alike. Even in quarters where the passing of the male breadwinner and his dependent wife are deeply mourned, recognition of political reality is unavoidable. In spite of some problems at the base, trade unions are prioritizing demands for a shorter working week, an end to regular overtime, and a decent basic wage. Equally important, some major trade unions are actively recruiting and organizing part-time, low-paid and contract workers. The worker of the future will either be, it seems, multi-skilled, full time, secure, well paid and male (and in a minority), or 'unskilled', part time, temporary, low paid and female (and in a majority). Generalizations apart, more and more people will move in and out of paid jobs according to the whims of the employer, spending periods of their lives on the dole queue.

This pattern is already reflected in trade union education. People employed on Community Programme Schemes (full- and part-time temporary jobs for the long-term unemployed), if they are union representatives, come on TUC shop-stewards courses. They are equally likely to join courses for the unemployed (especially if they are part time) as that is how they often (realistically) see themselves. Part-time workers attending TUC courses face some similar practical problems to unemployed students. The course timing is often unsuitable because of childcare responsibilities; and, because their work takes place at dinner-time or early evening, they have to rush off to meet the conflicting demands of family, education, and antisocial work hours. Finally, a part-time job usually means claiming a variety of state benefits and, as representatives, they must be just as familiar with the welfare benefit system as their unemployed colleagues.

Most of these problems stand in contrast to the routines and concerns of full-time workers in the same class. A Ford Halewood production worker attending a TUC shop-stewards' course in Merseyside (in November 1986), spoke to me about this:

> I didn't see what we could have in common with the bar staff and cleaners on the ten-day course. And it's true, their problems are different – much, much worse. But in one way I envy them. They've got something to fight for – a real reason to give people for joining a union. In our place people take what the unions have won for granted. They don't understand it can all be taken away.

> And it is being taken away at the moment. Talking to Sandra and Betty has made me realize how much we've got to lose.

To say that the educational needs of the employed and unemployed are similar is not to overlook some of the practical problems facing unemployed people. The unemployed are poorer, and if they are long-term unemployed are more likely to lack confidence and self-esteem. Nevertheless, the majority of adults left school with little or no confidence in themselves educationally, and never return to education. Whether employed or unemployed, they are easily put down, put off or left out. The experiences of adult educators referred to in this chapter (and in chapter 9) show that unemployed people are interested in all kinds of education, given the opportunity; and whilst their practical difficulties should be addressed (e.g. how to pay course fees and travel costs), it should not be assumed that separate provision alone will meet the needs of this varied and disparate group. As one unwaged woman attending a women's health course in Merseyside said:

> I went along to this course for the unemployed. The tutor did his best and the group were great, but it wasn't for me. I realised that although I'd love a paid job (I'm unemployed with two young children), I didn't think of myself as unemployed first and foremost. I changed to this course about women's health. It's great, and I'm learning new things all the time. Some of the women are unemployed, some have part-time jobs, but we've got a lot in common.[1]

Comments like these make a persuasive argument for bringing together the employed and unemployed. Unemployed people, too, require the resources of the trade union movement; as an unemployed worker from the Merseyside Unemployed Centre put it:

> As unemployed people, we need the support of trade unions. When our benefits are cut, who represents us? We can get individual advice, but who puts our case forward nationally and to the media? Trade unions are organizations for ordinary people, and they have power. We want them to use that power on our behalf![2]

And in return? There are many examples of TUC unemployed centres assisting trade unionists in disputes where their help is requested, especially where jobs are threatened. In recent years, Merseyside unemployed centres supported a worker sacked for reporting sexual harassment, contract cleaners sacked when the company changed the contractors, factory workers sacked for joining a trade union, and many, many others. Notably, during the 1984 NUM dispute, unemployed workers raised thousands of pounds for the families of striking miners. As a result of this and other less visible work, over 20,000 employed trade unionists on Merseyside make a weekly donation to the One Fund for All (the centres' fund-raising organization), often deducted from wages, along with union subscriptions. As a result, TUC unemployed centres have a real chance of independent survival.

Unemployment and adult education

It is not only within trade unions and unemployed centres that arguments about unemployment have taken place. Unemployment was a serious political and economic problem by 1979. In the 1960s and early 1970s it was recognized that full employment had not eliminated deprivation in inner city areas. Government and local authorities chose special measures, bringing extra resources to these communities as the way forward, but by the late 1970s, poverty and unemployment was on the increase. The 'you've never had it so good' era was well and truly over.

Adult educators have been quick to recognize their vulnerability. Always the poor relation of the education system, and with no statutory backing, the service was an easy target for cuts. Extra-Mural Departments (EMDs) and the Workers' Educational Association (WEA), long established providers of liberal adult education (and the Responsible Bodies nominated by the 1944 Education Act), received early warnings of future reductions in funds and changes in the formula for grant allocation. Further education lecturers could see themselves being squeezed between a reduced rate-support grant and the decline of their traditional day-release work. Emphasis on student numbers (Effective Student Hours, ESH, or bums on seats, in adult education jargon), money-making and popular courses looked like the order of the day. Agencies and individuals had to think twice.

From 1980 onwards, it was apparent that the government wished to make an educational response to unemployment. The question was – what kind of response and how would it link with the work of organizations already providing educational opportunities for unemployed people?

The Thatcher government was not alone, nor even a pioneer in this respect. There was, of course, a long tradition of formal and informal education for workers – employed and unemployed – within the trade union and labour movement. There was also a more recent tradition within and on the fringes of mainstream adult education that was supported and strengthened by the Russell Report's recommendations that more resources should go to the so-called 'educationally disadvantaged' – a theme echoed in other government reports during the same period.[3] 'Russell category' work was promoted within the WEA, by some EMDs, and by many voluntary projects funded by Urban Aid, partnership programmes and other similar sources. Whilst this work was rarely aimed at the unemployed as a category in the 1970s, it reached people who left school at the minimum leaving age and who would, in the 1980s, be particularly vulnerable to unemployment.

The education style and methods developed by these organizations are described elsewhere in this book. Here was the obvious starting point for an educational response to unemployment, based on and extending existing good practice.

In 1977, the Secretary of State for Education and Science established the Advisory Council for Adult and Continuing Education (ACACE). In 1981, it published a report on the public adult education service, introduced by the words: 'We saw no other sensible course except to start from extreme financial difficulties, affecting and in some areas disabling the service.'[4] A year later, in a second report, ACACE advocated a radical shift by the whole post-school education system towards the educational needs of adults.[5] It identified at least four sections of the population whose educational needs deserve priority for continuing education, not least because members of these groups are at present under-represented in their take-up of educational opportunities: manual workers, women, ethnic minorities, and physically and mentally handicapped people. It identified the key barriers to access as 'dispositional...institutional...situational'. It argued both for more resources and more care in the way education is made available to those excluded groups. Interestingly, the 'unemployed' as a category were neither identified nor made a priority.

This may be because the compilation of the report immediately preceded the leap of unemployment up the political and educational agenda; for it was in 1982, the year that the report was published, that the era of the 'special project' began.

So what was the government strategy, and why did it fail to build on existing good practice? Before answering this, it is worth referring to a few lessons learned by those WEA districts and EMDs that received funding for the three-year projects.

The WEA's approach, as expressed in its manifesto on the subject, was to stress the wide-ranging educational needs of the unemployed and the importance of building links with key organizations.[6] The WEA stressed the extra difficulties facing unemployed women and black people, and the importance of any educational provision for the unemployed reflecting a positive and central commitment to those groups. Work carried out in Leeds revealed that a systematic and well-organized programme of education for the unemployed attracted unemployed people even in the early stages. In Edinburgh, the WEA had developed a full-day 'New Directions' course for the unemployed. In Swindon, the WEA tutor organizer preferred a project-based approach, focusing on practical and creative approaches.

I have already outlined the Merseyside experience, which has much in common with this kind of work. If there was a difference, it was that the educational programme was more firmly located within the trade union movement in general and the TUC education scheme in particular. This said as much about the nature of that movement as it did about the adult education organizers and officers involved.

From all this activity, common features can be identified, and a flexible model of good practice can be constructed. The key elements of this model can be summed up as follows: fee provision, a wide choice, partnership with organizations involving and representing unemployed people, an understanding that 'the unemployed' are not a homogeneous group (and certainly not all white men), active and participatory teaching methods, and a willingness to face up to controversial and challenging social and political issues.

Government strategy

In March 1984, under the heading 'Jobs for the boys on jobless programme', *The Times* reported:

> The DES took the adult education world by surprise on Monday with its announcement of a £2.5 million programme over the next three years – to be known as Replan – to improve educational opportunities for the adult unemployed.

According to the report, only a quarter of the money would be spent on development projects, while most would be spent on appointing regional field officers to 'disseminate good practice' – hence the newspaper headline. The Open University was to produce distance learning materials in the form of survival packs to help the unemployed in tackling the immediate practical problems of their situation and in exploring the options open to them in the future. It was envisaged that some of the money would be spent on counselling and guidance with special reference to coping on a reduced budget, handling redundancy money, do-it-yourself skills and low-budget catering.

Reaction from other adult-education agencies was not positive. Robert Lochrie, general secretary of the WEA, whilst expressing his astonishment that voluntary agencies, trade unions and WEA elected members had no representation on the scheme's steering committee, was quoted as being

> extremely disappointed with the sum available for development projects and strongly suspected that the £2.5 million was not new money at all, but had been cut off the grants to the WEA and EMDs – the very people who were struggling to provide services for the unemployed.

The report was followed by a footnote stating that the government intended to withdraw its annual grant to the Educational Centres Association, whose leaders had been told that the Association's 'participatory style of education was unwelcome'. The Parliamentary Under-Secretary of State, Peter Brooke, noted that

> further progress could be helped by a centrally funded development programme, involving the evaluation of innovative forms of provision, the identification and dissemination of good practice, and the mobilisation of all relevant interests, including voluntary agencies, who are anxious to help.

Both the National Institute of Adult Continuing Education and the Further Education Unit were to play a part in grant allocation for the fund; for 'Replan', as the new scheme became known, was an attempt to get adult educators to rethink and replan their services and resources in order that the unemployed might make better use of them. As a result, it was suggested, the unemployed themselves might replan their approach to the problem of long-term unemployment.

There were many reservations expressed by adult educators about Replan when it was launched: it was cosmetic, temporary, and underfunded. The most serious and least understood criticism of the scheme was its individual approach. The unemployed person had an individual problem (unemployment), for which there must be an individual solution. The stress on 'how to cope with reduced circumstances', self-assessment, and 'acting on unemployment: personal change' (as included in the Open University material), suggested a benign version of the old adage, 'pull yourself up by your bootstraps'. (To be fair to the OU, their material also included sections on social support, unemployment in context and acting on unemployment.) The thrust of the DES proposals was away from participation and towards an education that would keep the unemployed on the margins of society, individually working out solutions to problems not of their own making. The emphasis on distance learning compounds such an interpretation.

However, as sometimes happens in matters of policy implementation, the practice of Replan was considerably better than its theory. This was not the result of high-powered advice and support from the government, but because many organizations, once they had accepted that Replan was a fact of educational life, made applications for funds. Development work with the unemployed went on in WEAs, voluntary groups, and EMDs based on and extending past good practice. Now most Replan development projects are winding up. Projects were funded for a maximum of two years and applications for extensions have been refused. Workers who have scarcely established themselves are now charged with the task of leaving something positive behind them. As the regional field officers finish off and produce their portfolios of good practice, the policy-makers regroup. Replan has served its cosmetic function. Leaflets have been produced, conferences successfully organized. What happens to this work is a side issue.

However, unemployment has not gone away, and further visible initiatives are needed. Reflecting the increasing role of the MSC within education at all levels, the most recent government initiative placed education alongside training and temporary employment schemes in its programme 'Action for Jobs – Restart'.

How does this new scheme work? All long-term unemployed people, initially in certain pilot areas, are called in for interview to their local jobcentre with the aim of getting them off the dole. Options offered might be a suitable job, a temporary job on a government scheme; a place in a job club; the chance of self-employment; a place on a training scheme; a £20 per week top-up for accepting a low-paid job; voluntary work; or a Restart course of one or two weeks for the unemployed person to assess what s/he is good at and to learn how to look for jobs more effectively.

At the time of writing, colleges of further education are scrambling to set up the lucrative Restart courses, using both existing staff and special temporary appointments. Other agencies such as the WEA and TUC unemployed centres have been approached. There are many objections to Restart – not the least of which is that it is locked into government proposals aimed to prop up low pay. Similarly, the threat of a withdrawal or reduction of benefit where co-operation is refused is repugnant to claimants and adult education alike. Compulsion is, to say the least, outside our tradition. Surveys carried out by the Low Pay Unit indicate at least 2,000 claimants ceasing to claim benefit. Early experiences of people attending the five-day Restart courses were described in an article, 'Five wasted days', in a Merseyside magazine, *Counter Claim*, in the autumn of 1986:

> On the first day we were...also told to fill in a silly questionnaire – the first of many which asked things like 'What's the worst thing about being unemployed?' and 'One good thing about being unemployed is...'
>
> They also gave us 'fact sheets' about the problems of being unemployed. One of them contained the following gem – 'There are those who find it difficult to make ends meet, while others seem to get used to managing on benefits.'

In Restart, education has taken on a different meaning; it has, too, less apparent importance to the government than their training/employment strategy. With this in mind the great debate about education for the unemployed may slip down the political agenda, which gives adult educators the chance to get back to basics.

Conclusions

In outlining the way in which the government has funded education for the unemployed since 1979, I have possibly overstated two obvious facts: firstly, that decisions about what type of education is best for 'the unemployed' have been made on the basis of moral panic and political expediency, rather than professional judgement; secondly, in a social system based on market forces where unemployment levels are unpredictable, there is a risk that the unemployed only get resources when there are lots of them and they feature on the official statistics – when unemployment is not at the forefront of public concern, or where the unemployed are invisible, they are pushed back to the margins.

It seems important, then, to plan a system of education for adults in which the unemployed are centrally included. As I have been suggesting, it is also desirable to think creatively about how education can bring together employed and unemployed workers, especially where the trend is towards a labour market with a relatively small core workforce, and a majority of workers moving in and out of temporary jobs and contract work.

My own experience in Merseyside suggests, too, that it is vital that education for the unemployed should be organized primarily with and by trade unions and the TUC. Trade unions, after all, represent the largest pressure group within our society; but the ability and willingness of trade unions to be active in this way depends partly on their own policies and rule books as regards membership qualifications. Trade union centres reflect the imbalances of the wider trade union movement, with a majority of male, white members; and unemployment has tended to look like a male issue, caught up in ideas about the breadwinner. Positive action policies in the education programmes of unemployed centres are beginning to change this, however, with an increasing number of women's courses, and recruitment of more women and black tutors.

The TUC scheme can and does bring together unemployed workers nominated by their unions and offers access to wider union courses. A widening of this scheme based on active and collective teaching methods and building on people's direct experience, if it was properly funded and resourced, would provide the basis for a long-term and secure educational facility for the unemployed. Of course, many unemployed workers will not be and may never have been trade union members. For them to have access to education in the same way as employed workers, a system similar to Italy's '150 Hours' (see chapter 10) would make some sense: that is, one in which unemployed people would have free access to courses for employed workers. The extent and variety of their opportunities would not then depend on attitudes to unemployment – but on the basic commitment of the government of the day, perhaps backed up by new legislation, to support an adult education system for all adults.

6
Adult literacy: Campaigns and movements

Jane Mace

A holiday for education?

It's seven o'clock on a Wednesday evening in an upstairs room in Anycity Literacy Centre. By nine o'clock there will be nine people in the room (four black and five white). At this stage, there are four: Joan and Bill, tutors, with Olive and Jake, students. Both Olive and Jake come regularly to this class. Olive has worked for nine years as a clerical assistant in an oil company. Jake is out of work at the moment; he was made redundant from his job as heating engineer four months ago, and got a new job with the council only to discover he was expected to write daily reports on his work schedules. His hope, in joining the class, was to do a crash course in writing in time to keep up with this new demand on his skills and avoid losing the job. This had turned out to be impossible; he had left the job, taken on casual work, and was still looking. Olive, as a black woman in her forties, was more confident than Jake in her writing but on too low a scale in her firm to be eligible for promotion (let alone the in-service training that would get it for her) and came, each week after work, in order to do what she could to develop her self-confidence in her own education. She had also attended, for the last six months, the maths class at the same Centre on a Monday night (and taken time off work, the previous winter, to attend a five-week course for women on computers, organized on Friday mornings).

Late arrivals that evening were Neil, Maria, Delroy and Anthony. Neil completed a two-year course as a mature student the previous year to qualify as a community and youth worker, and now worked in an intermediate treatment centre. Daily reports, minutes, and letters, put considerable pressure on his tentative hold on spelling and grammar in the job – something he had tried to work on during the course, but still felt a need to develop and practice. Maria, an Irish woman in her thirties, had joined the class only that evening, with the anxiety of an impending interview for a job as a home help. 'My spelling's hopeless', she said; 'I know I could do the job, but I might crack up if they ask me to fill in a form there and then.' Anthony, aged 17, had recently left school, and found reading hard, writing harder. Delroy, a hospital porter, had rejoined the group after two months' absence visiting relatives in Jamaica. The last to join the group was Annette, a young black woman student of teacher training, who was one of the Centre's new volunteers, visiting the class as a preliminary to joining it as a voluntary tutor.

Neil had to leave early, to pick up his 8-year-old child and take him home to bed. Olive always had to leave on the dot of nine, in order to catch the bus home (some twenty minutes ride, then ten minutes walk). Effectively, then, the total group of nine people were together just for one hour. Of the nine, just six were students – yet on the register for this class are twelve names. The previous week, seven students were in the class; the subsequent one, four. In a twelve-week term, only three students were able to come every single Wednesday evening.

This brief sketch describes fairly accurately the reality of much of what goes on under the name of adult basic education in this country. It's the job of adult-education tutors to try to create, in an hour or two a week, the possibilities for varied groups of women and men with limited 'spare time', money and energy, to grab hold of something called literacy. Tutors like Joan, Bill and Annette do what they can to tune in to the individuals who turn up that evening, offer ideas and resources for working on their reading and writing interests, and enable them so to interact that when they leave, they have gained some small change in what they believe they can do. The students may bring with them, as Anthony did that evening, a letter he was writing to a friend; or, as Olive did, an idea that she wanted to discuss (that night she came in, sat down, and began asking what we knew about civil law). Like Maria, some come with an event they want to prepare for. Many others, like Jake, Delroy and Neil, bring less specified learning to do. All bring with them, into any class, a wide range of personal, social, economic, political and emotional experience.

In just that one hour when they are all there at the same time, there is the opportunity for an exchange of some of that experience. Literacy tutors, as groupworkers, learn to think on their feet. The prepared materials for that evening may have little to do with the themes that emerge from conversation – about the traffic, last night's news, or Olive's interest in the law. As it happened, that particular evening, after several individual conversations and pieces of writing had been worked on, everyone spent some forty minutes together discussing a piece that Bill had brought in from that day's local paper on the subject of the next royal wedding. The question discussed was: should the day of the wedding be a national holiday?

What does a 'day off' mean to someone who is unemployed? What could a 'public holiday' mean to a worker in the Health Service, which depends on 24-hour staffing, 365 days a year? Of what interest are the family celebrations of a rich white family to low-paid black workers? The discussion that evening, raising these questions from the personal circumstances of people in the room did something to remove the sticky taste of that week's sugary media coverage on the subject. As each student then wrote something of what she or he had said, both students and tutors offered support and strategies for dealing with the technical job of spelling and grammar that arose. Listening to each other read back the result was a means to reassemble and reaffirm the different points of view in the group.

As this chapter suggests, opportunities of this kind have been growing in literacy education over the last fifteen years, and there has been a positive effort in some places to democratize the process of learning – with positive results in the growth of collective consciousness and confidence. What it also underlines, however, is the grotesquely limited resources, given these possibilities, being offered to mature adults such as Maria, Olive, Neil, Anthony, Jake and Delroy.[1] Achieving the right to paid time off work to study is a vital means to extend those limits; although, of course, to those like Jake, Maria and Anthony, who do not have jobs, such a right would not offer any immediate change in itself. The chance of being paid while studying full-time would. Payment – whether as grant, training allowance or wage, collective control of learning, and the power of writing as a means to release group and individual potential: these are the three themes of this chapter. They also recur throughout the book; but they weren't always present in the literacy campaign in the 1970s.

Campaigning for the literate consumer

In the late 1960s and early 1970s alarming reports began to appear in the press of a phenomenon in this country called 'adult illiteracy'. In 1969, I was one of an early wave of volunteers who surfaced in response to what, then, was still a limited appeal for help in resolving the problem, becoming a tutor with the literacy scheme based at Cambridge House Settlement in London. (I went on to work there on a paid basis, first part time, then full time, for another nine years.) By 1973 a campaign group had formed and for the next three years local and national journalists wrote features on the issue in the press and for radio or TV, enjoining more volunteers to offer help. During the same period, by a coincidence of interests, politicians and professionals concerned with the education system were confronting the sicknesses there – not least of which was adult education's failure to attract working-class people to its doors.[2]

An emergency was declared. The then Labour government persuaded itself to release a central fund of £1 million to bring aid to the disaster area. The BBC mounted a series of programmes intended to speak to the isolated individuals in their sitting-rooms and persuade them to seek the help they so evidently needed. A target date for 'eradicating' the illness was even aspired to (though it has since, unsurprisingly, been forgotten). The confident hope was expressed that by 1985 'the incidence' of illiteracy 'could be reduced to a fraction of the present level' (then estimated at two million adults in the country). 'At the end of this period, there could be a fresh plan geared to eradicating the remainder.'[3] Thousands of volunteers were recruited and trained. The campaign was positively messianic.

For some reason, however, its message never took hold in the organized labour movement. Mass literacy never then, or at any later stage, sufficiently captured the imagination either of rank-and-file trade union members or our leaders to acquire the status of a manifesto. In this book we wish to argue that entitlements to paid educational leave offer one means by which opportunities for educational growth can be placed in the hands of working-class women and men themselves. We are suggesting that it can only effectively be done by those people being in charge of the circumstances of such rights and such education. In thinking about how this could be done, there may be some lessons to learn from the early literacy campaign and the various manifestations of a literacy movement which followed it.

What was it that in those years of a major revelation of education's failures prevented this issue from becoming a central concern of the trade union movement? It is my hunch that one answer to this is fairly simple. Unions, at least in theory, are about unity, uniting with a common cause. The business of trade unions is to combine, to give mutual support and to resist, as a collective, any attacks on their members. The *practice* of adult literacy work, as it evolved over the next ten years or so, grew to be a lot about grouping, collecting and working together. I'll come to that later. In its earliest stages, the *campaign* was, above all, about individuals.

Ideas about illiteracy, both in the 1970s and today, tend to centre on male illiteracy. The image has been, more often than not, that of the isolated man, locked in a personal sense of failure, unable to get or keep jobs because of the inevitable form that had, sooner of later, to be filled in. The female image, when portrayed, depicted the mother tragically unable to read to her child or buy the right can of soup. Both, as well as being about individuals, were images of a consumer culture. Both perpetuated an idea of literacy as consumption. Both, in short, stressed the difficulties of the 'illiterate' in reading. The efforts at national and local level to stimulate a response to this phenomenon – quantified as 6 per cent of the adult population – mimicked this set of images. Government and local authorities were urged to provide funds and training which assumed a personal, confidential, private approach. A major proportion of the effort was devoted to 'recruiting' volunteers. It was accepted that these would need some form of training, and funds for training trainers, for training conferences for volunteers, were allocated across the country. The volunteers, by and large, were expected to carry out the teaching in their own or their students' homes, using resources they put together at their own expense, and often paying for travel costs to and from classes themselves. The volunteer literacy tutor, in short, was (and in many parts of the country continues to be) an unpaid homeworker.

Trade union leaders, to the extent that they were moved to add their voice to the campaign around adult literacy, tended if anything to collude with the construction of illiteracy as a pathology, requiring personal prescriptions, as distinct from a social, economic or even class question.[4] At the 1975 conference on 'Literacy at work', convened in London by the National Committee for Adult Literacy, Jim MacGougan, General Secretary of the National Union of Tailors and Garment Workers, reported that the General Council of the Trades Union Congress 'pledged its support for the campaign' for adult literacy.[5] There was, he said, 'a moral obligation' to assist, since 'it is wrong to allow any section of our community to be disenfranchised by ignorance'. The idea of a 'moral obligation' incumbent on the literate majority was echoed in an article from another member of the TUC General Council, Dougie Grieve, writing three years later in *Labour Research* of the 'very clear duty' before the trade union movement to help its members with literacy problems, publicize the courses, and keep up a pressure for adult literacy classes to continue.[6]

Dougie Grieve wrote that article after taking part in a Saturday conference in south London in 1977 on literacy and the trade union movement. It was organized by literacy workers in voluntary organizations and further education (members of the Southwark Literacy Development Group, which continues to be an active local co-ordinating body) and sponsored by the Southwark Trades Council. The sponsorship was agreed at a meeting of the Council in July that year, following a speech I made to it as branch delegate from my own union, NATFHE (National Association of Teachers in Further and Higher Education). Our branch, at that time, like many others, was acutely aware of the economic marginality of literacy work, precisely at a time when that work was being given most visibility in the media. We were conscious, as trade unionists ourselves, of the pressure that meant for our own jobs; a pressure which was made more acute by the daily reminder of the pitiful provision which we could offer the women and men who came to our centres as students, alerted by this very publicity. In raising the issue in the forum of the local Trades Council, and taking on the planning of a conference for trade unionists sponsored by the Council, we were, I think, trying to create, at a local level, another kind of publicity, one based on shared assumptions that the 'causes' of illiteracy were to do with class, not personal inadequacies. We were trying to shift the burden of euphemism.

The conference was not successful. Barely a dozen people turned up. In Manchester, that autumn, a similar event was initiated, also from NATFHE trade union members who were literacy workers.[7] There may have been others. None, in any case, were on a scale that could begin to challenge the dominant media versions of 'educationally subnormal students', 'non-readers...groping around the alphabet in a fog', or 'adult illiterates...in a shadowy secret world'.[8]

'Write First Time': a group without a leader

Meanwhile, however, earlier that same year, another conference took place, in Derbyshire. Sixty-four people came. In financial terms, it was sponsored by the government-funded Adult Literacy Resource Agency.[9] In concept and execution it was actually sponsored by another grouping of people altogether: the dozen or so members of the 'Write First Time' collective (of which I was one). We were all tutors. Thinking about it now, I would think all of us, too, were trade unionists (it was hard to find any paid literacy workers then who were not); but the conference was not a trades union event. Its funding had been granted on the basis that it was 'training', on the basis of a residential weekend. The reason it was important then, and remains a landmark now, is that the concept of the event was that half the participants would be literacy students.

Until then, the ALRA's support of such events (and there had been many) had always assumed that the people who should be encouraged to attend training days, courses and weekends, were the teachers/tutors, and those who were to train them. The Write First Time group, in applying for funds for accommodation costs and fares subsidy for 60 people to attend a national training weekend, stipulated that 30 of them should be, not the 'professionals' (or aspiring professionals), but the students – conventionally seen as the subject matter for training, but not its beneficiaries.

It was, then, a *conference*, with all the amenities (accommodation, good food) paid for, and a fares 'pool' (which meant that no one paid more than £3.50 to be there), open, for the first time, to working-class, low-income, educationally unqualified, mature adult students of literacy. For most of those who came it was the first 'weekend away' from their families they had ever been able to experience. Being released from the anxiety about finding the money for it, they were released, also, (particularly the women students) for two days and nights from the demands and needs of those they lived with. What they were coming to – a conference – was a meeting of equals; not a holiday, exactly, not work, in the usual sense, and not even 'education' in the morally acceptable sense of 'self-improvement' to which many adult students of literacy feel bound. Yet, in some sense, it was an occasion which is a mixture of all three. The kind of occasion that professionals go to all the time.

The second important feature of that March weekend in Derbyshire is that 'the subject and the object of the weekend was writing'.[10] The title of the conference was 'Writing and its place in literacy work'. We who had organized it chose this purpose for the event with an experience of publishing, by then, some eight issues of the paper called *Write First Time*. Begun in early 1975, with an idea about filling a gap in suitable reading materials for adult learners, it was edited by a collective of tutors from Liverpool, Sussex, Bedford, Brighton, Manchester and London. The writing we published was not by tutors, however. Each issue printed some thirty pieces of writing sent in by students of literacy. Our conference in March 1977 was an effort to gather some of those writers and readers together to explore ideas about writing. What happened, in the event, is that a lot of time was spent on discussing the production of the paper itself. As a result of the questioning and discussion and energy of that weekend, this process of production was changed. The writing, as always, would be student writing. The editing, managing and producing would begin to be shared out with other people – students, as well as tutors – and each issue would be made by a different local group – with support from members of the existing collective.

For us on the collective it was an outcome for the weekend that we had not anticipated. It was exciting; it was also rather frightening. Over the next eight years (until 1985, when our last application for grant aid was turned down, ending the publishing activity) we learned, often painfully, that if we were to run meetings that made sense to *everyone* who came, whether they could read and write or not, a lot of things had to change (the writing of agendas and minutes, the checking of apparent consensus, the dominance of those who felt confident in meetings over those who did not – and so on). In class terms, the members of the Write First Time group from 1975–7 shared some common ground with members of the earlier 'Right to Read' campaign group, in 1973–5, who were, as Marietta Clare, a literacy worker in Leicestershire, has pointed out, by no means a representative body of working-class literacy students. The 1974 Right to Read document, in her words, was 'produced by self-styled literacy specialists' (of the British Association of Settlements).[11] The originators of Write First Time, albeit practising teachers of adults, were in the same category. This time, however, in the attempt to create reading material that was of adult interest, the central concern was that the material should be written by writers on an equal footing with the readers – namely, the literacy students themselves, writing from their own diverse experiences and sharing a common political position. What was to become Write First Time's principal claim to fame, then – the assertion of the potential of literacy students to be producers, rather than passive consumers of literature – emerged from a conscious policy to publish writing by these other 'literacy specialists'. Until the 1977 conference the editorial control remained with the teachers (who often, interestingly, prefer to describe ourselves as 'literacy workers'); but as the editorial in the last issue of the paper put it, from then on the change of policy meant an important change in practice:

> As students began to make the paper, they also joined the Collective. This was the first time that adult literacy students could meet

each other across the country, on a regular basis, with their fares paid. . . . No one has more say than anyone else in meetings. It's hard work sometimes, and it bothers some outside people. They don't know who to send letters to, for example, and they think that a group without a leader can't know what it's doing. But we have found it's worth working at in its own right, and have thought up a number of ways to run meetings so that newcomers can understand what is going on and have their say, too.[12]

Write First Time effectively created a new set of dynamics between writers and readers. Its readers became authors of other publications:

> I wrote this book because I want people to come forward to learn to read and write. I want the outside world to know that literacy students can write. I spoke to students and tutors from several schemes. I explained that I wanted them to tell me what other literacy schemes are like, and what it's like at work if you can't read and write. I tape-recorded students, and tutors typed it out. I wrote a lot myself, too.

That's how Isobel Bowie's book *Through the Door* begins.[13] As a student at Blackfriars Literacy Scheme, Isobel Bowie had attended a local writing weekend held a year after Write First Time's 1977 event. The booklet of writings by the weekend participants had included a piece she had written.[14] Reading issues of *Write First Time*, as well as the growing number of writings published by other projects, had stimulated her, like many others, to believe her writing was worth reading, too. This opening to her own book is written with the confidence not only in her own validity, but in her position as representative of others. It's one of those words, 'confidence', that keeps appearing in talk and writing about literacy; Isobel Bowie's confidence in addressing the reader – and in interviewing the students for her book – could not easily have happened if she had only learned in private, on her own. Originally, she, like many others, had worked alone with a personal tutor; but later she became an active member of a class at the Centre and, as she tells us in her book, a member of the Literacy Scheme Committee.

Some time after Isobel joined a group, Alison Tomlin took on a job at Blackfriars with ALRA funding to develop daytime work with the scheme; and from November 1976 until April 1978, she set about trying to achieve paid release for existing students who had daytime employment to come to classes in worktime. As the grant was not renewed, it was not possible for the work she did at Blackfriars to be continued there; but the NUPE Basic Skills Unit, which was later named Workbase, took its origins in part from the initiatives Alison Tomlin was able to make (see chapter 7). Contacts through students, approaches to local employers, and links with four trade unions (NATSOPA, SOGAT, TGWU, and COHSE) resulted in a number of local women and men being released in work hours to attend daytime classes at the Scheme. Southwark Council, Trust Houses Forte, and St Thomas's Hospital catering department all agreed some arrangements for employees to have, usually, four hours a week release to develop their skills in literacy.

Literacy and politics

A year later, in 1979, at a national conference of the newly formed National Federation of Voluntary Literacy Schemes (NFVLS), discussions on funding and organization of voluntary projects included an interesting paper presented by Alison Tomlin about the difficulties of creating honest and useful structures for students to 'manage' the schemes and projects they attended. She referred to the 'essentially paternalistic history' of the student committee at Blackfriars Settlement, and spoke of the 'constant worry that the Literacy Scheme Committee only rubber-stamps the paid workers' ideas'. One 'wider question' which she identified then, was the importance of avoiding 'token gestures'. As she saw it, 'the development of users' management of literacy provision' should not only be a means for users to acquire more 'confidence, etc. and the skills to cope with formal meetings', and have a greater say about how and what they learned. These are important reasons. If they were to be the only reasons, however, she argued, such committees would only be 'a front to make "straight" literacy more palatable'. The development of users' management of literacy provision', she concluded, 'should be seen as part of a political struggle for democracy.'[15]

The way in which literacy education interlocks with issues of training, paid leave to study and a sense of collective confidence clearly takes on entirely different meanings in different political and economic contexts. In Nicaragua, for example, illiteracy in 1980 was estimated at 50.2 per cent of the population; after the overthrow of a dictatorship, there was a revolution to build. It is little wonder that in such a setting, the language of a literacy campaign should be rich in military metaphor. (The campaign was described as 'the cultural insurrection', and the 'second war of liberation'.) Literacy and political struggle in the national literacy crusades of Cuba, Mozambique and Guinea Bissau, too, were seen to be inseparable. As for literacy training on a PEL basis, the strategies in such a setting are interesting. Both training programmes and the literacy classes themselves were held in the evenings and weekends – to ensure that the work of the peasant families could continue. At the same time, the literacy *brigadistas*, school and college students who were normally the economically inactive sector of the population, contributed much-needed extra labour in the job of harvesting, planting, and care of livestock in the rural areas, without occupying jobs that could have been taken by Nicaragua's unemployed.[16]

'Last year I took up a gun; this year it's an exercise book', a 17-year-old literacy worker in Nicaragua said. Here in Britain, literacy education was run for twenty-five years on a paid-release basis in one unexpected quarter – the Army. From 1959 until it was closed in 1984, at the barracks in Corsham, Wiltshire, the Army School of Preliminary Education ran ten-week courses for those recruits who were seen to have weaknesses in their English and maths. Jane Lawrence, a literacy worker carrying out some research in 1980/1 reported on a visit to one of the SPE's open days. The purpose of the Army's literacy courses was 'to raise the educational standards of adult soldiers who have basic educational weaknesses which prevent them from benefiting fully from normal military training' (the five months' basic training for all new army recruits). Each course took eighteen recruits. (So, in twenty-five years, at a rough estimate, the SPE must have trained some 2,500 recruits.)[17]

Learning literacy in the Army meant, as Jane Lawrence also reports, learning reading. No written skills, she was told, are either needed or taught, except for the most limited of creative writing tasks, that of taking messages. All the learning was highly structured; soldiers worked individually in the 'reading lab' and had their work marked by the officer instructor. No self-assessment of progress was seen to be necessary, and no groupwork either.

Neither guns nor exercise-books are neutral weapons. The Army, wishing to maintain an obedient and submissive body of men (and the SPE never ran any programmes for women) understandably excluded writing from the syllabus. By contrast, in Nicaragua, the teachings of Paolo Freire (whose work was first available in English translation here in the early 1970s) and the political goals of the crusade, meant a recognition of the power of authorship. Peasants learned to write in order to become active in the collective struggle. Write First Time's 1977 weekend was described as 'training', basically, for reasons of expediency at the time. (None of the other work of producing issues of the paper by groups in Blackburn, Bristol, Birmingham, Dorset, Dublin, Manchester or the many other centres which took part in the activity over the years was ever, as far as I know, so described.) Yet the experience those meetings and workshop gave to both students and tutors could be said to have been very much a training programme. Just as Isobel Bowie developed her sense of consciousness both through writing and through participation in the committee, so other women and men, coming together with a sense of something they are in charge of – making a magazine of their own and other people's writing – acquire the sense of belonging to a group which commands recognition.

The National Federation of Voluntary Literacy Schemes, founded in 1978, is now a network of over eighty centres and projects across the country, with an office in London. One of its main functions continues to be the development of training in the voluntary sector. Since many of its member groups were located in centres with the kind of 'paternalistic history' which Alison Tomlin referred to, the question of 'management', participation in committee structures, appeared early on in the organization's concerns. An interesting feature of the work in recent years has been the weekend national and regional conferences and workshops, open to students and tutors alike from their member organizations and planned, always, by groups of volunteers, students or tutors again, for some months in advance. Neither students nor the tutors (whether part time or full time) are awarded PEL for these meetings or for the weekends; but two essentials remain to make these events accessible: a fares subsidy and crèche provision.

Confidence – a feeling of freedom

Meanwhile, in the same year Write First Time began (1975) the Manpower Services Commission initiated the only full-time courses in basic education that have ever existed in this country, outside the Army. The Preparatory Courses were targeted precisely at those whose difficulty in numeracy and literacy prevented them getting and/or keeping employment. They ran, initially, on a 48-week year, in further education colleges and adult-education centres. Trainees could participate on a roll-on, roll-off basis for as long a period as felt necessary up to that maximum. In 1976 there were 400 trainees on such courses; by 1977, 1,544; but times were changing, and so was the MSC. Guidelines issued in 1980 marked the beginning of the end. From then on, only those who seemed likely to be able to reach 'a required standard' at the end of thirteen weeks could be accepted. In a minority of cases, this could be extended up to twenty-six weeks; but the average stay on the course had now to be 13–18 weeks.[18]

For anyone trying to reclaim a new sense of themselves as an active and literate individual, the difference between being a spare-time member of a part-time group, and being a paid, full-time student, is considerable. Gerry, a man who had experienced both, put it like this:

> Part-time classes were very good...But there's no comparison with coming two nights a week after working all day. For me it was so basic, I'd be coming for the next ten years, coming two nights a week, to get as far as I am now...It's only now that it's starting to flow into place.[19]

Brighton Friends' Centre, a voluntary organization with a long record of basic education provision, in 1975 achieved MSC sponsorship for a 36-week full-time Preparatory Course (a total of 1,260 hours) open to adults wishing to develop their education in maths, literacy and general studies. There was, indeed, 'no comparison' between what, till then, was the only opportunity they could offer for literacy education ('two nights a week', or the equivalent) and the opening these courses represented. Those who got a place as 'trainee' or student on them were eligible for the same training allowances paid to those attending the range of more 'advanced' TOPS courses also sponsored by the MSC, (see chapter 3). Against the increasing pressure in job interviews and applications for evidence of basic English and maths, many women and men found the chance through courses such as this to regain a sense of their own potential and abilities.

Outside the Army, these, then, were the only full-time basic education courses that have ever existed in this country; but by the end of 1985, MSC funding at the Friends' Centre (as elsewhere) supported, no longer courses that were full time, for eight or nine months, but short, 10- or 12-week part-time courses (with no training allowances for the students). The 'targeting' policy of the early 1970s, by which specific social groups were singled out as worthy of MSC training to enable them to enter the labour market more effectively, was over. The 'work preparation programme', as one regional report had it, 'should cater for everyone's needs' now.[20] As one writer commented:

> It seems paradoxical...that in 1976 the Preparatory Course at Friends' Centre in Brighton consisted of 36 weeks of full-time provision...yet in 1985 *when the number of adults unemployed has more than doubled in the area*, Job Link Courses (the replacement of the former Preparatory Courses) are for 12 weeks, part-time (a total of 240 hours). [my italics][21]

Signing Off was the title chosen for a 20-minute video film shown at the Friends' Centre in January 1986 to a large public audience. The production group for the film was a group of some eight students from the 1985 Preparatory Course, who, with course tutor Annabel Hemstedt, worked with a local community video project to put together their own argument for a quality of education which these courses, to them, represented. The group had interviewed ex-students and their colleagues on the course just ended. Each told of the importance that the course had had in their lives. John, who opens the film, begins with a definition: 'Confidence. To me, confidence is a feeling of freedom. An extra piece of ground to walk on, unfettered.' Sue, a woman who we are told 'gets up at 6.30 every day' in order to get to the course in time – having two children, and a husband to see to before her twenty-mile journey to the Centre, says, 'For me, the course has given me tremendous confidence.' Kath refers to the breakdown which had made her 'completely forget everything I'd ever learned', and says that for her too, the course 'gave me back my confidence'. Roger, Paul, and Sanja each tell us what they have gone on to achieve in terms of employment and further training.[22] It's a biased film, because it is a campaigning one; but this time, the campaigners are speaking for themselves. Its producers are also its subjects.

Part II
Paid release in practice

7

Workbase (London)

Mary Wolfe

Background: 'Part of our lives, naturally'

> As far as I was concerned, the course made me confident the Union was trying to help. Since then, I tried to start another class, but I had to give it up, which was difficult. If you work all day, in the evening you want some time for yourself, or to talk to the children. Anyway, most times I am working from noon to 9.00 p.m. and the other class was from 6.00 to 9.00 whereas in worktime I was able to go. Courses like this should be held in our worktime, not when we're too tired to learn. It should be part of our lives, naturally.

The speaker is Irene, a shop steward/care assistant employed in a local authority home for the elderly. She had completed a course in adult basic education in worktime, organized by Workbase, Trades Union Education and Skills Project, two years previously.

Over the years at Workbase, we have developed our strategies in response to a wide range of particular circumstances and objectives. While there have been mistakes, difficulties and compromises for all of us, we have also seen emerge methods which reflect the specific nature of learning basic skills and of operating within a working context. This outline describes some of the developments in the work so far as it is perceived by people who, in different ways, have been actively involved in moving basic education right into the working lives of students. The men and women whose words are recorded here spoke to me both during the preparation of this chapter and at different times over the past years. Their comments highlight some of the different strands involved in siting an education project within the students' workplace. Nonetheless, this is an individual reflection on what I hope will continue to be a varied and evolving type of educational provision.[1]

The project began in 1978 when the University of London launched a new employees' training programme which was to include an increased provision for its manual workforce. Until this time, training for support staff in the university had often been restricted to task-oriented short courses responding to particular work situations such as equipment maintenance and First Aid. There was an evident irony in an organization dedicated to improving standards of higher education simultaneously relying upon the servicing support of a group of employees, some of whom had enjoyed little or no further education since school. The adult literacy campaign of the time had certainly raised public awareness of educational inequality and the local officers of the union, the National Union of Public Employees (NUPE), had recognized for some time that the limited basic skills of some of their members remained an unspoken issue which was largely unresearched and unappreciated. They discussed with the training officer how an opportunity for workers to take up basic skills classes could be agreed on the basis of the same payment and conditions already granted for work-related training for other grades of staff. An initial agreement was reached for the extent of the need to be examined in certain areas, and for basic literacy and English language support classes to be provided in worktime, without loss of pay, in response to the interest expressed by the manual workforce.

It was originally intended that graduate teacher-training students would be invited to act as volunteer tutors for employee-students, either on an individual or a group basis. This scheme had the attraction of providing useful learning to the student-teachers and of using the university's own resources fully. What it did not address, however, was the reluctance of employees to volunteer for courses taught by the young students whose rooms they cleaned, nor of locating the classes within a traditional workplace framework. In the event, the lack of any direct recruitment strategy meant that the programme remained a principled agreement rather than a reality. For this hoped-for reliance on volunteers failed to recognize the crucial importance of a vital component in setting up successful basic education classes at work: face-to-face outreach work. As I shall suggest later, this preparatory work not only acknowledges the stigma of illiteracy feared by workers applying for training, but also ensures that individuals' skills and experiences are respected and used in the ensuing classes.

With hindsight, it is perhaps easy to understand how much more straightforward it was for the union to negotiate the right to classes than to ensure the practical implementation of the scheme. This is not to belittle the achievement, since the agreement undoubtedly raised an awareness of the effects of educational discrimination not only with the employer but also among the union's own officers and members. Nonetheless, the union's experience of education was rooted in its own and the TUC's training for employee representatives, which remained primarily geared towards the massive demand for courses in health and safety, bargaining skills and shop-steward training. On the other hand, the employer's training programme was dominated by the pressure to meet the needs voiced by its technical and managerial staff. Neither group had the experience or the facilities to assess or cater for the particular demands of Marie, a cleaner who had never been to school, nor of Olga, her colleague and a graduate whose limited English prevented any real contact with her co-workers.

The classes did become a reality when the trade union approached local adult educationalists for support in organizing and teaching the courses. The unions and employers concerned then formed a team working with paid tutors employed to organize and teach the courses in the newly-formed NUPE Basic Skills Project, later renamed Workbase. The Project received a grant from the Adult Literacy and Basic Skills Unit in what was to be an exciting new alliance of adult literacy tutors, trade unionists and employers, co-operating to realize adult literacy as a right and not a privilege. Indeed, it seems now that the early development of the scheme from the initial recognition of an unmet need, through inadequate strategies relying on volunteer tutors, to the establishment of local groups with paid teachers, demonstrates precisely the strength to be gained from workers' organizations combining with the campaign for improved adult literacy provision which, it has been suggested, was missing in the early 1970s (see p. 82).

Equal opportunities: 'It's not a favour from them'

Whereas the first agreement to run Workbase courses, in the University of London, was reached in the context of negotiations specifically around training, subsequent agreements have recognized the contribution of such courses to the implementation of equal opportunities policies.

At first, the need to provide classes at work was recognized as part of the employer's acknowledged responsibility to provide literacy/ESL courses as a legitimate component of a wider training scheme.

This purely training context for the scheme highlighted the underlying tension between the aims of the employer and of the students which remains an issue in PEL courses. It's not surprising, then, that the 1983 report of the early programme should list its effects as ones which would appeal most of all to managers and employers:

— improved industrial relations arising from this education provision on-site;

— increased awareness of the need for clear communications among all employees;

— greater understanding of the role of health and safety regulations;

— more confidence amongst trainees in carrying out written instructions;

— clearer understanding of workplace systems, such as holiday or bonus payments;

— increased participation in the workplace as a whole by trainees.[2]

Persuasive as these arguments may have appeared, they characterize the employees as the cause of the difficulties identified rather than recognizing the systematic oppression which creates the problems faced by many workers. However, when basic education classes are agreed within the context of an improved equal opportunities policy, the focus shifts away from an implication of employees' weaknesses to an affirmation of their potential. Basic skills courses make an essential contribution to such programmes, now repeated by a growing number of public-sector employers, which overtly address the realities of discrimination in education and training; but, because of prevailing attitudes which persist in equating illiteracy with stupidity, the offer of basic education does run the risk of implying a deficit in the worker: an implication that is not there, for example, in the invitation to join an effective management course. As Betty, a cleaner, put it to me:

> I know that when my supervisor goes on a course, then it is because he's doing well in his job. I'm not here because I'm slow but because classes like these should be in our working contract and management should know it's not a favour from them. That way, more people would take up these educational opportunities.

Shirley, an Equal Opportunities Officer, recognized the affirmative value of promoting a course which, as she told me,

> could not be directly about jobs, but about providing more opportunities. It has been an exciting experience, involving us all in the process of opening horizons. I know the catering manager was suspicious at first, but because he became engaged in the whole process he was very receptive when courses for his staff were put to him and he felt a sense of purpose in becoming involved.

As Jane Mace put it, in her book, *Working With Words*, eight years ago:

> A lot more people have to wake up to the consciousness that they have a responsibility to the grown men and women whose lives are hemmed in by the bureaucracy they can't understand, employment openings they can't take, culture they can't make theirs. . . literacy students are the people who have the courage to ask for help in learning. . . in making words work, in working at words until they make sense, until they carry meaning from the head to the paper, from the paper to another head, and beyond.[3]

Outreach: 'At last we were seen to be taking something seriously'

Since the project started, Workbase tutors have discussed the opportunity of joining workplace classes in literacy, numeracy and ESL with over three thousand manual workers employed mainly in the public sector in London. Approximately six hundred employees have subsequently taken part in courses, usually in groups of 6–8 students attending for an average of 150 class hours. Each of these courses has been preceded by group and individual meetings between tutors and prospective students. These discussions focus upon the aims and uses of the courses, based upon the student's own view of her employment, educational and domestic experiences. They have taken place at six in the morning in half-swept offices, next to noisy machinery on night-shifts, in cloakrooms, kitchens and park-huts. The first meeting might take place in a dayroom of a residential home for the elderly. A care assistant keeps her eyes on the group of people around the television and tries to describe to me her educational experience and ambitions. For both of us, it is hard to imagine the reality of her attending a class during paid worktime.

As a tutor, this outreach work which necessarily precedes working as a group in a classroom (or conference room, or canteen) is at different times interesting, threatening and complicated. The prospect of asking a woman cleaning the corridor to interrupt her work for twenty minutes to share her feelings about booklearning, her frustrations, her countless responsibilities and interests, is rightly a daunting one. As one of my colleagues described it: 'The early interviews are always tiring because you're like a sales rep. You need to be teaching as well to get the balance.'

In a context where training opportunities have been systematically denied to the very people we are now seeking to interest, this individual approach seems to be essential, for, among many manual workers who, over the years, have applied for promotion or training without ever receiving a reply, there is an understandable level of cynicism. In our interviews, then, it is important to stress that these courses will happen. They are not for the officers who do the desk-work but for those who 'only' make the beds and help the elderly to bath, who do the cooking and the laundry and all the other undervalued and essential jobs. Obviously, not all manual workers need or are interested in a return to education through their workplace. Many employees, who are not interested in the particular training we offer, have used these initial discussions to find out more about other training courses provided by their union, employer or local education centre.

It is also crucial to be able to reassure future students that their confidentiality is guaranteed, both in this first conversation and in any future course. Men and women who, often since the age of 14 or 15, have worked long hours for little pay have a real fear of losing even that work if they have never had time to keep up their formal writing skills. One student, a plumber, speaking to me of his embarrassment about being unable to read a central heating manual, was reluctant to recognize his own skill in being able to install a heating system without a manual. We can provide this guarantee of confidentiality because Workbase is an independent organization, not part of the employer's hierarchy.

On average, the process of meeting the senior trade union representatives and managers, the departmental supervisors and shop stewards, then of arranging employees' meetings and meeting each individual worker, takes perhaps three to four months in a section of a hundred employees; longer when we have to wait for funding or approval from council committee cycles or area committees. None the less, this time spent learning, explaining and negotiating does two other things. It teaches the tutor the feel of the workplace: the pressures, loopholes, allocation of work and actual hierarchies; and, as the two people quoted below suggest, it provides status and credibility to the training.

> I feel the fact that we employed an organization specifically to talk to part-time women cleaners about training was an assertiveness exercise in itself. At last, we were seen to be taking something seriously. (Mary, women's unit officer)

> It was good the way that lady came down to find me in the morning. Usually this building is empty apart from me, so I hadn't thought she'd find me. In the end, we had a cup of tea together and that encouraged me to take part. I told her I'd had no education at all: I never could go to school a lot because of my mother being ill most of her life. All I learned was from newspapers and bit by bit I'd taught myself to read and write but not very well. Anyhow, I took the confidence to apply and I thought my course would start in September. When it didn't start I just thought they had swept it all under the carpet like a lot of other things, but then we got going in January and there were six other women in the group. It made me feel something was being done. (Ellen, cleaner)

Part of the job? 'We could be called back to work'

Despite the apparently specific nature of the courses Workbase offers, we have seen a high level of interest from members of the manual workforce. Obviously, manual workers' educational needs or interests are no more uniform than those of any other section of the community. Equally, basic education is a phrase which tends to confuse more than it can clarify. Certainly, it cannot adequately reflect the wide-ranging interests, demands and skills brought to their classes by students. Different groups have, variously, tackled the forms required to claim statutory sick pay; examined the power relationships reflected in different map projections of the world; practised spelling and arithmetic; compared the effects of traditional and technological health care; read about early trades unionists and requested meetings with their local MP at the House of Commons.

The subjects considered in many classes reflect the interests of the learners as workers. The students have a real interest in understanding their working conditions fully. Hence it is necessary to know how to use a calculator before understanding a wage-slip which expresses hourly pay to six decimal places. Tackling the intricacies of formal English is a necessary precursor to assessing the merits of a bonus scheme. The classes also provide the support and space needed for the women and men taking part to compare their experiences, to write about their lives and read their own history.

One result, as Aileen, a catering worker, reported, can be an increased sense of recognition awarded by others:

> I have been here for years, and it really changed my life starting those classes. I did not achieve that much – I achieved a bit but it is not really what I achieved, I have found myself a bit of comfort. Since my first course, I have started at the college next door and the Administration Officer was interested in how I was getting on – she asked if my course had started and I said yes. So a few weeks ago she came up here and asked if I was still going and how I was getting on. I said it was all right and you know in all those years it was the first time she'd ever asked how I was getting on. Really – nothing whatsoever: you just do your work upstairs. So, I've found somebody who is interested. She is very nice, you know.

As a pilot scheme, Workbase offers us, as students or tutors, freedom from time-established patterns of working. It also presents a sometimes frightening lack of familiarity. The fact of being within the students' workplace, rather than in a more traditional adult education centre, still evokes in me some hesitation about finding myself on someone else's territory. Yet, just as education at work begs a number of questions about what kind of activities we include in our definition of work, so too the physical surroundings of our classes invite a reappraisal of where we site education. 'Their' territory needs to become 'ours' if education is to become part of the job, rather than a spare-time activity ostensibly offered to those workers with the luxury of time to spare.

There are contradictory issues around where to hold paid educational leave classes. Since we are showing that education is part of the job, it is important to stake our claim to facilities and space at work. However, there are also practical difficulties preventing us from holding classes within the actual workplaces of some students:

> I couldn't come if it was in the Home. There are too many people there wanting to know what we're doing – I couldn't relax with people asking questions or interrupting us. Anyway, I think it would cause difficulties if there was a rush on – we could be called back to work or feel we shouldn't leave the job. (Lynette, laundry worker)

In general, the solution seems to be to hold classes in the usual conference rooms or workplace training centres. We are thus securing our right to use training resources while providing the necessary privacy and space away from the immediate pressures of a busy job. Having coffee and biscuits provided in the training room represents a welcome change of role for the students who are normally employed in servicing the traditional users of these facilities.

On a practical level, the methods of recruiting manual staff to basic education classes at work necessitates from the first an approach which recognizes the students' status and vulnerability as employees. There is no guarantee that opening the door to education at work, and particularly to a programme of basic education built upon the personal achievements and interests of the students, does in fact give the correct status to these achievements. Often, in-service training courses are advertised through broadsheets which appear and disappear seemingly randomly from notice-boards; information on TUC courses is circulated to branches where it can remain hidden in the inevitable pile of correspondence at meetings. The resulting impression is that manual-worker training is directed towards those employees who are able to attend branch meetings regularly, to read notices, complete forms and perhaps even to negotiate their training-time individually. Carol, who for thirteen years has left home at five o'clock each morning to clean the offices of unseen members of the white-collar staff, summed up her understanding of workplace education: 'I didn't think training could be for us people – it always seemed to be for the big people.' The freedom to learn at work is a unique opportunity to combat the often isolated working conditions of many students. Employees enrolling on courses see their efforts validated by their union's and employer's support for them.

In talking to women about their own early hopes of careers, I have shared in a pageant of often unfulfilled ambitions. Flower-arranging on ships, office work, nursing, brewing, teaching and football coaching – few of the women would have chosen paid work as cleaners were it not for the prior demands of their families. Some now feel ashamed of work which for them has little status or value, some have retained a determination to 'get on' and secure for themselves, sooner or later, 'a job with a title'.

The information which we have been privileged to share during our meetings to set up new programmes has demonstrated clearly the need to establish basic education classes for manual workers within initiatives for enhanced equality of opportunity at work. Three Local Authority workers, all involved in local courses, summed up this view.

> We approached Workbase, I suppose, because it was there as a package. Providing paid release for manual workers was radical –

so the links with the trade union movement were key in establishing the programme and certainly the reality of discrimination against manual staff, as a group, made sense to the union. And to give employees a sense of their worth we needed to start with the lowest-paid workers: the part-time cleaners and the caterers. We wanted an altered strategy of training, so that training wasn't just for your job, and that was where basic education fitted in. Many manual workers know they are distanced from the educational system, and it was important not always to say you should become a clerical worker but to show a pride, now, in people's work. It's amazing the lack of control many women face in their jobs: the school-meals workers who have no say in dietary policy or the home helps who are never consulted about their rotas. Basic education didn't offer an individual solution to the undervaluing of manual workers, and particularly of women, but it did make us all look at the position in general. (Judy, equal opportunities officer)

When I sit in on an interview for the union – some applicants you can see that they do lose out. I really feel there should be more on basic skills: the council has got this equal opportunities policy so they should be doing something, working jointly with the unions. Recollecting my own course I think I can speak out more openly, and I have got more confidence: I learn more, even writing a letter now, and it helps a lot. I think we should learn more about how this policy works because my members still feel it's not coming into the workplace. My members feel they should be treated fairly and it is not happening at all, just look around . . . We feel we have so many problems so the council should feel it has an obligation to run these courses. (Lesley, shop steward, care assistant)

With the equal opportunities policy, whatever you are you know you should be treated the same. It isn't true but they just say that. It should be, but it isn't. Maybe for some people it is true almost, but for some people it isn't. We work in the kitchens, we'll never have equal opportunities with the lecturers. . . If you can manage to go to college and you're ambitious, well – it's good. Maybe for myself, if I continue, I'll get more confident. (Karen, catering assistant)

Negotiating conditions: 'If my bin doesn't get emptied'

Effective facilities for cover, as suggested in chapter 2, are vital if PEL is to avoid belittling the value of manual work and implying acceptance that such work can safely be left undone. We have needed, in Workbase, to win the recognition that attending a programme of study forms a productive part of work. The results of education do not remain as individual benefits for the learner, but contribute to the ability and confidence of the whole workforce. In one sense, describing this particular kind of work as PEL is unhelpful. The trade unionists, tutors and employers who accept this campaign for basic education at work are claiming that learning basic skills is, in itself, a legitimate form of work. The trade union movement's own educational provision has already given respect and credibility to the experiences of working-class adults as a sound qualification for formal study. By extending this provision to include the opportunity to acquire or brush up basic skills, we are providing a forum which supports education as a right and which can constitute a confident challenge to the present monopoly of PEL enjoyed by white-collar staff.

Our own position as a trade-union-supported project allows us to work with, and influence, initiatives coming from within the organized labour movement to increase equality at work. Equally, the progress we have jointly achieved in securing paid release from work for manual workers is of real benefit to the membership as a whole. Once access to basic education becomes a priority on the trade union agenda, we have seen the membership become more active and more confident in claiming the right to cover for their jobs and a more equitable share in paid education schemes. Alex, a shop steward, told me:

> I'd been active in the union ever since I joined the council so I knew most of the problems we faced with overtime and holiday schemes. It wasn't until we got these classes started that I learned much about the problems some of the ladies are facing, so for me it's been a real learning experience. One of the ladies told me she'd never been to a meeting because all we did was to talk about the bonus and she wasn't on bonus. That made me think a bit.

Insidiously, the present climate of cutting back jobs in the public sector presents a real threat to properly organized training. Fred, a union branch secretary, was well aware of the risks:

> We're being asked to lose 120 jobs from the school-meals service. If any of the women there were to go on a course – say leaving four in a kitchen, not five, then management are going to try and get rid of that fifth job.

The disturbance which PEL implies to management may appear to be little more than a temporary inconvenience, as an executive officer in local government put it to me:

> I know the other managers will be as committed to this scheme as I am – after all, it's council policy. And if it means my bin doesn't get emptied quite as often, it's the price we'll all have to pay.

We'll all have to pay. . . ? Without adequate cover, the price paid by the cleaner to attend a class would be a vain attempt to stretch her part-time hours even further; for the kitchen assistant, putting her only paid employment in jeopardy. Both employees are faced with an erosion of their job satisfaction. However, when employee representatives use the framework of their negotiating machinery to win recognition for basic education programmes, they confirm students' rights to acquire the skills they need with confidence and dignity.

Summary: 'It's my turn and I'm going to take it'

The very openness of a PEL course focusing on basic education has served to demonstrate that the need and desire to improve writing and maths as an adult are not marginal. The employers, tutors and trade unionists involved have often expressed concern over the possible offence which may be caused in offering programmes of basic education.

In the event, this sense of resentment has rarely been voiced by the workers with whom we have discussed the scheme. Almost all the workers I have spoken to have direct experience of colleagues who are frustrated by unequal access to education:

> I was on a health and safety course at the college. First thing we had to take notes. This lady said she couldn't spell – she just said that straight off and I think that took some courage. There's people I know bring in letters for the supervisor to read. So, it's not right, it's embarrassing to go about your life like that. (catering assistant)

There is a danger that basic education courses at work may become a low-status offer to low-status workers. However, as a provision which is complementary to a full manual-worker training scheme, basic education recognizes both the generally inadequate training provision available to this important section of the workforce and the recurrent pattern of discrimination which has threatened a proportion of that workforce in their access to schooling, jobs and training.

While it is important to ensure a place within mainstream training for those people who are concerned to improve their spelling, maths or English skills, it is also important to learn to recognize and respond to the wide variety of other training needs expressed by manual workers. Many of us who are involved in winning the right to paid educational leave for basic education have become more confident in voicing our demands for reasonable standards of cover, accommodation or release time. Undoubtedly, the outreach work we do before starting a course does raise expectations among the great majority of workers we meet. Many people who are not interested in a basic education course have been encouraged to apply for other training and many people who discounted themselves from formal learning have completed Workbase courses. Obviously we cannot raise these expectations unless there are established strategies to meet them. We are thus involved in broadening the scope of manual-worker training as well as in contributing a particular programme of basic skills. Equally, just as the educational outreach work allows the time and support sometimes required to voice demands and expectations, so students completing courses regularly see the programme as only the first stage in securing their rights to a fair share in adult education and training, as Clara, a catering assistant, did:

> I thought I was too old to start learning, but basic skills gives you confidence. I am much more interested in things than I used to be...This course wasn't long enough so I will apply for a catering course now. At first, I thought a course would not be for me, now I think there should be more courses for us – I know I can enjoy it, after all I've seen all my kids to college: now I feel it's my turn and I'm going to take it.

Having developed our confidence in asserting our demands more clearly for education at work, as part of work, we need to extend these demands to include meeting those hopes and interests developed in returning to learning. One hundred and fifty hours – the equivalent of four working weeks – is very little when compared with the time given to professional training or with a working life spent servicing other people's needs.

For the future, we need to continue to demonstrate that an improved provision of PEL necessarily involves including basic education in our demands. Far from being a marginal issue, it is central in ensuring more equal access to education. Many of our strategies – the central role of the unions, their links with employers, the outreach work and counselling provided – may prove equally useful for PEL schemes in a wide range of areas. If basic education is to become an accepted part of an overall training programme, it cannot remain entirely within the voluntary education sector. Rather it should seek to ensure a statutory place in the training departments of employers and other schemes. In London a small but growing number of public-sector employers are taking on their own staff to continue the work formerly contracted out to Workbase. Provided that these schemes continue to recognize that training in basic education is as much an employee's right as is training in new technology or in supervisory skills, then this is a positive advance in the campaign for paid educational leave. The trade union movement can ensure this recognition by maintaining their involvement in monitoring, supporting and extending schemes designed to enhance the skills and opportunities available to members.

8

Take Ten (Sheffield)

Cathy Burke, Graham Birkin,
Steve Bond and Maggie Norton

We were suspicious of the leaflets inviting us to take a day off a week for ten weeks. It was strange to be asked to study subjects which interested us and could be of our own choosing. What was it all about? What was the Gaffer's angle – giving us time off with no obvious advantage to him? We who swept the city streets, cleaned toilets, did the filing, mowed grass verges, and the numerous humdrum, irksome, important, but under-valued jobs which have to be done by that ill-fated proverbial 'somebody'. No-one ever gives us 'owt'. We were wary, but we took a chance.

Were we going back to school – a place we had gleefully left at the ages of fifteen or sixteen? On reflection, it was a stranger experience than we had bargained for. We were expected to investigate all sorts of social problems, and where possible did this in a practical way.

For example, we had the opportunity to visit places we would not normally have seen: a centre for drug addicts, an assessment centre for mentally handicapped, the police headquarters, and places in the news, like Broadwater Farm (in Tottenham, London), and Toxteth (in Liverpool). We were able to meet key people and discuss problems at first hand.

We had 'professional' speakers who gave us information on trade unions, race relations, law and order and nuclear power. The talks were always followed by questions and lively discussion. We were provided with sources of information we would not have had otherwise, and stimulated to think about things in greater depth.

We were encouraged to discuss and explain our own jobs. By exchanging ideas we gained a deeper insight into the working of the local council. We found that many of the manual workers' frustrations were shared by clerical workers: we had a lot in common.

Some course members who usually work in an all-male environment were at first ill at ease at being in a mixed group. We already knew about equality of the sexes – or thought we did! However, for many of us it was an enlightening experience. Through our discussions we began to realise that discrimination affected us all, particularly women and black people. By working together, we gained an understanding of complex problems. We became conscious of prejudices we didn't even realise we had!

So in the now-stagnating city of Sheffield, a flickering candle has been lit. Men and women are taking part in paid educational leave, which releases them from the tedium of dead-end jobs taken only as a last resort.

We are being taken seriously. PEL has given us encouragement, confidence and time to share experiences and knowledge with our colleagues. It has re-affirmed our faith in human nature and proved that the 'community spirit' is not dead. It has given us the ambition to want more.

That piece of writing came from some twelve hours of collective work, not as part of 'paid educational leave' but in the evenings, outside work time, as a voluntary activity.

We had sent out a letter to a number of ex-Take-Ten course members, asking them to come to an evening meeting to hear about the plans for a book on PEL and to make a contribution to the chapter on the work in Sheffield. About a dozen people came, and ten of them made a further commitment to meet and write something together.[1] Their enthusiasm for writing was partly a result of some of the work they had done on Take Ten, for as we shall show later, writing is an important part of each course. Some of them had been on Take Ten during the pilot stage: they had thus been away from the scheme for almost three years and time was spent comparing what had happened then with what was happening now. It was a good example of the kind of education Take Ten professes to be: collaborative, critical, supportive and geared to a practical outcome. For us, the tutors, it was part vindication of the value of the scheme.

But what is Take Ten?

Broadly speaking, it is a ten-day programme of release over ten weeks for Sheffield City Council workers. The target group is those workers with no post-school qualifications and, as a priority within that, the low paid. Its objectives are outlined in the publicity leaflets viewed with the 'suspicion' referred to earlier. Here we quote from the Women's Course leaflet (that for the mixed courses is similar, but omits the references to changes in women's lives, part-time work and health. It includes a reference to 'how and why Sheffield has changed'.)

With TAKE TEN you can

* learn how the Local Authority works, how your job fits in, and what it means to local people;
* find out about ways to change things at work and in your neighbourhood;
* work together to gain confidence;
* look at how our lives and the choices we can make, as women, have changed;
* find out about your rights as a part-time worker;
* have more information about your health;
* think about how to make the most of your abilities and where to go from here.

The four of us are employed full time by the adult education service. We teach and develop the courses with the support of a part-time clerical worker. Our working week is usually taken up half with teaching and half with curriculum development, some recruitment, course planning and administration.

The scheme runs two mixed full-day courses and one half-day women part-timers' course per week. The mixed courses last six hours, from 9.00 a.m.–4.00 p.m., and the women part-timers' course, four hours, from 9.30 a.m. to 1.30 p.m. Two men and one woman teach each mixed course, with a maximum of thirty-six course members. The women part-timers' course is staffed by the two women tutors, and takes a maximum of twenty women. So, each term there are three courses running, which means that over the year about 270 workers come through the scheme.

Recruitment is primarily the responsibility of training officers in the Central Personnel Department. It is they who make sure the leaflets and posters are sent to all the worksites, using both departmental and trade union channels. They then organize worksite meetings where the tutors can talk about the scheme. Quite often workers come to such meetings with no clear idea what to expect, and it is difficult to explain Take Ten in the 10–15 minutes available. The meetings are most successful when workers have already heard about the scheme from their colleagues: personal recommendation is always the most effective method of recruitment. The fact that workers apply for places on the course direct to Central Personnel is important: it cuts out some of the favouritism which can operate in the workplace itself. They do not have to ask for anyone's permission.

Each mixed course is as far as possible made up of an equal number of women and men. Sometimes this is hard to achieve, as fewer women apply or get release for these courses than men. In our experience there are several reasons for this. A woman's commitment to her work, her colleagues and her clients is relied on and often unwittingly abused by the manager or supervisor. She may be made to feel guilty about taking time off for education. Dedication to the work, no matter how low paid and repetitive, may prevent her from applying when she knows management will not provide adequate cover. Both inside and outside paid work women have less opportunity than men to take time for themselves. As a result, many women have very low levels of confidence when it comes to education. The Personnel Department and the tutors have thus had to work particularly hard to ensure an equal balance of women and men on the mixed courses, and a steady recruitment of women for the part-timers' course.

Once release has been gained, course members first meet each other and us at a two-hour 'preliminary meeting' in the town hall, where the aims and methods of the course are discussed and any practical difficulties of getting there dealt with. The courses themselves start the following week.

What goes on in a Take Ten course?

The courses take place in an old school building, a short bus-ride away from the city centre. To one side are the sites of demolished steel factories; to the other, some of the city's experimental 1960s deck-access housing. The building itself has the forbidding air of any Victorian Board School, but inside the atmosphere is relaxed and friendly. The courses are based in a set of rooms linked by a coffee and library area. We have controlling use of these rooms and so have been able to decorate the walls with changing displays of course members' work, photographs and exhibitions.

We prepare an agenda of times and contents of sessions for each day of the course and usually give it to course members a week in advance. Each agenda is built round a theme, decided by the tutors for the first few days, and with the course members later on. The issues looked at during the first few days of the course are built on workers' demands to know more about the council, its decision-making processes, and where their jobs fit in. The general approach may change from course to course, partly because of our need to change and improve methods and partly because of changes in the political context. For example, at the height of the council's campaign against rate-capping in 1985, course members could connect work done on the budget with the campaigns organized at their workplaces or in their communities. The issue had a relevance and an urgency which was lost when the council set a legal rate. A year later, the same session was still interesting but it was more difficult to relate it to everyday concerns at work and at home.

THE MORNING GROUPS

A safe place to write

The only constant part of the timetable is the first session in the morning when a small group meets with the same tutor each week. These 'morning groups' are intended to be the 'safe' groups where, because of familiarity, members are more likely to open up and take risks, either about admitting they are not understanding aspects of the course, or about themselves and their personal lives.

It is during these sessions that most of the writing is done – quite often in spite of members' original intentions. We always have to overcome feelings of technical incompetence in reading and writing – feelings which are often translated into having nothing worthwhile to say. For many, technical incompetence and personal creative power become muddled until they are experienced as one and the same thing. Starting from talk, we move on to discussing detail in the safe atmosphere of the morning groups. Personal writing comes in as a way of storing valuable talk.

Of course, few people expect that the course will involve such considerable time and effort in writing and listening to other people's writing. Very few, in saying that they would like to improve their writing skills, imagine that personal writing will become any part of the process. Quite a number feel perplexed by our enthusiasm for writing, feel ambivalent about it and go along with it just for the sake of a quiet life; a few feel very threatened. The fear of being checked, judged and compared with others once they put pen to paper is deep-rooted. Yet with many, by the end of the course, the barriers are down and the struggle is rewarded by a pleasure and pride in seeing their piece, alongside the others, in printed form.

A time to negotiate the curriculum

On the mixed courses, these morning groups choose two group members to represent the views of the group to us and course members in the other morning groups. Often these course representatives chair sessions or take on particular tasks like explaining the agenda at the beginning of the day. They change at least once during the ten days, usually after the 'planning exercise' which takes place round about the fourth week.

By this time, members are confident enough to consider or suggest issues which they might have fought shy of at the beginning of the course. Working initially in the morning groups, the course representatives find out what course members want and then meet together to present perhaps a list of nine issues to the group as a whole. At the end of the exercise the group negotiates a shortened list of two or three issues with us, the course tutors; we then say what we feel to be the advantages and disadvantages, practicalities, etc. of the chosen issues. The introduction to this chapter gives some indication of the range of topics this process has produced. As it also suggests, the methods used on the course are aimed at enabling students to be as active as possible, by means of visits, information gathering exercises, short discussions, reporting back, interviewing, photography and role-play.

Skills, on the whole, are picked up on the way, through immersion in topics. Some skills in other contexts would be called 'study skills', like taking notes, or gathering information, but because we emphasize working together, these individual skills take on the public, collective aspect of being able to say what you want, or to work effectively in groups. (When we talk about notetaking, for instance, we stress how powerful the act of notetaking can be in situations where it is not expected – when a worker is at issue with her manager, for instance, or when a woman goes to see her doctor.) In fact they become part of 'political skills'.

Where did Take Ten come from?

The idea for 'Paid Educational Leave' – as Take Ten was simply called at the beginning – came out of a general concern in the early

1980s within the Sheffield Labour Party to open up local government, expressed in a series of informal discussions which led to a range of initiatives all based on the notion of 'building from the bottom'. Some adult education workers were involved in these early discussions, and it was their particular contribution which led to the notion of paid leave which was not strictly job-related.

The council, under the new leadership of David Blunkett, was developing distinctive policies for the running of its services. A number of councillors wanted to counter the negative effects of years of paternalism on both the workforce and the public. Better communication with the workforce and better relations between those who ran the services and those who used them were all key concerns. In the face of further central government cutbacks and a general undermining of 'local democracy', David Blunkett talked about council workers becoming 'ambassadors for the council', understanding the issues and arguing the case (for Labour) wherever they came into contact with the public.

The adult education workers, from the local authority education department, the WEA and Northern College, were not convinced that such a close link between the political needs of the Labour Group and a PEL scheme would be either desirable or effective. The workforce had many grievances and might be wary of councillors courting their support. Being an 'ambassador' made no sense to the low paid and those constantly denied any influence over work organization. If it was to be successful, PEL had to be part of a process designed to help manual and clerical workers understand their situation and the ways to change it.

These initial discussions 'went public' in a seminar called by the Central Policy Unit in December 1982. Entitled 'Adult and Continuing Education Policy in the Local Authority and the Community', the seminar involved representatives from the trade unions, management, adult education and councillors. The main address was by Keith Jackson, the senior tutor at Northern College, who argued that PEL should be seen in the context of the need to return the thinking about, planning and controlling of services to those actually providing them. The seminar had top political backing. Blunkett introduced it and, in the months immediately following, made sure its recommendations were acted on. As a result, within two months the Policy Committee had endorsed the idea of a 'programme of continuing education on a paid-release basis' – for *all* its employees, and later agreed on a pilot programme to give priority to manual, craft and clerical workers.

The Policy Committee set up a Curriculum Development Group (CDG), whose task it was to turn abstract principle into concrete programme. It included representatives from the trade unions, the Personnel and Education Departments, the Central Policy Unit, and tutors from adult education and Northern College. The latter, with its residential adult-education work, had the experience of combining the best of trade union education with community action and structured learning; and the adult-education service, with its emphasis on democratic, participative and collective styles of work, was ready to establish that combination in a day-release setting. The trade unions, with their knowledge of steward and membership education, stressed confidence-building, collective skills, and 'getting things done'. They were concerned that the programme should not stay within a closed circuit of education for its own sake, but lead course members outwards, to increased participation in trade union and political activity. Thus, three different educational organizations, with their different backgrounds and resources, put together a programme which was different from any existing models of PEL.

By September 1983 thc CDG appointed four tutors and, by October, the first course members joined the scheme. This speed of implementation, coupled with the fact that the scheme was, from the start, 'employer led', meant that more unions felt that they were being pushed into accepting a programme about which they had doubts. Tensions and suspicions were eased by making a distinction, early on, between the right to, and terms of, leave (to be dealt with by union negotiating officers), and the programme for which leave was granted, including tutors and other resources (to be dealt with by union education officers through the CDG). Full-time union officers wanted this distinction to be absolutely clear before the pilot scheme was converted into a permanent one, and it was agreed that the Personnel Department of the council would administer the scheme (organizing release, pay and cover).

So although the scheme was not formally under trade union control, trade union officers did in theory have considerable power. On many occasions they were asked to make an input into the curriculum, but in practice, their own internal organization made it hard for them to do so. Only three of the unions involved had full-time education officers, and they had a large region to cover in which the Sheffield Take Ten scheme was but one of many concerns. NALGO had a lay education officer who could get time off for meetings, but none of the other unions had a system of lay representatives. Some key council unions like UCATT (Union of Construction, Allied Trades and Technicians) and COHSE missed out on the curriculum discussions altogether, and in the end only four unions were relatively well represented in the CDG during the first three years of the scheme (NALGO, NUPE, GMBATU and TGWU).

Obviously these institutional arrangements are crucial in that they largely determine what kind of PEL is on offer. Without union involvement, PEL could easily degenerate into management-led training. This might not necessarily be job specific, but could be general in the sense of seeking to extend a worker's range of transferable skills, in preparation for the 'flexible working practices' of the future. Union involvement makes sure that PEL is not hijacked for management purposes, and links it closely to the notion of workers' collective interests and advancement.

But *how* the unions are involved is also important. In Sheffield there have been times when the balancing act between the two Local Joint Committees (the negotiating bodies for the manual, craft, and white collar unions), the CDG, the Personnel Department, the Education Department and ourselves has not been easy. One of the reasons for this has been the difficulty of keeping everybody informed via the complex structures of local government; another has been the variety of educational traditions – and expectations – brought together at the CDG. Sometimes we were all using the same words but meaning different things.

For instance, as adult education workers we always stressed that Take Ten was an 'adult education course' – that is, was not trade union membership education, or a form of personnel training, or in any way linked to management. We felt we were following a tradition that went back through the work of Tom Lovett in the 1970s, the WEA, the Labour Colleges, to groups of workers learning together in the nineteenth century. For us adult education *was* non-elitist, participatory, and democratically controlled.[2] But for others 'adult education' had a different ring: of imposed courses, academicism, 'middle classness', which compared unfavourably with the styles and methods developed in trade union education.

Of course, the proof of the pudding is in the eating. At the end of each course, members make out a group report which is then taken by course representatives to the CDG. These reports have constantly stated that the methods used were not 'like school', that members had plenty of say in what happened, and that there was collective rather than competitive learning. Representatives have said all the things which could be said of a trade union education course (except that all course members would now be active or more effective in their unions). But getting the reality of the courses over to members of the CDG has been hard work, and if there is one lesson we have learnt over the years it is that all of us involved in the scheme should have spent more time in the early stages looking at our different educational traditions, and being clear about our styles, methods and aims. The different interests represented would not have melted away but at least we could have prevented some of the mutual misunderstandings.

Take Ten as committed and partisan education

Because of its political origins and content, Take Ten has been viewed with mistrust, too, by some representatives of council management, and some potential course members. Critics have caught on to some apparently provocative curriculum item (the nuclear debate, Broadwater Farm, Liverpool City Council) and concluded that the courses are simply political propaganda designed to consolidate the position of the majority group, the Labour Party.

These political overtones have also worried some trade unions, albeit for different reasons. Although on the whole sympathetic to the politics of the scheme, they have felt reluctant to endorse the

sympathetic to the unions might use a similar scheme for anti-union purposes.

Much of this distrust stems from a misunderstanding of what ‘political education’ *is* for Take Ten. As we've said already, the early idea of making council workers ‘ambassadors’ was soon dropped, together with other propagandist intentions; but if the scheme is not propagandist, then neither is it liberal education, even if that tradition includes a commitment to critical discussion and to advocating individual participation in political processes. Our approach is to go further, by practising these procedural values within a framework of equality and co-operation, and to stress that real change can only come about by collective organization and action. For our intention has been to establish a particular set of substantive values, some of which can be developed from existing elements of mutual self-help found among any group of workers; but others (for instance, anti-racism and anti-sexism) may require a wider political perspective.

We are thus both *committed* in the sense of upholding certain values and ideals rather than others, and *partisan*, in that we start from the standpoint and interests of the working class. Given the variety of people within the working class, it's not always clear what these will be. On housing, for instance, there may be a clear class position (e.g. there should be more of it) – but not on crime. So these broad intentions cannot be mechanically applied, and may sometimes evaporate into not much more than sympathies. They do mean, however, that every issue is tackled in the context of class power and inequalities, and that we are not neutral between the powerful and the powerless.

So we make a distinction between commitment and partisanship on the one hand, and propaganda (which implies manipulation and passivity) on the other. Adult education as practised in Take Ten means encouraging people to question, be sceptical and criticize. Of course there is a link between these procedural values and our personal politics: we hope a scepticism against received opinion will be matched by a similar scepticism towards those in power.

In studying 'how the council works', for instance, course members, as employees with sometimes as much as 25 years of council work behind them, can share the experiences they have of the organization which employs them. This 'common subjectivism' has to be discussed and made accurate with additional information. Often there is a difficult leap from the world of experience to criticism and evaluation; and the leap is even harder when course members are asked to consider different viewpoints to their own. The only way to do it, as we see it, without damaging a course member's self-respect or losing her/his interest, is to affirm the value of what each person brings to the course, and show how, in a very real sense, it is the prime source material for study.

This is particularly true when the topic is likely to be contentious. Here is how one of us described how she and a group of course members began to tackle racism:

> We were a group of eight, including myself and the one black member of the course. We were four men and four women, and ranged in age from 19 to 60. We met over three weeks, spending a total of seven hours together. My objectives were limited: to try to come to an understanding and definition of the terms 'prejudice' and 'racism', and then to look at some aspects of racism in our daily lives.
>
> I had already prepared an outline of the first session. We began by saying why we had chosen this option. A variety of reasons were given: a need to understand prejudice; concern with problems in the inner city; racist attacks and fear for the future; wanting more knowledge of the council's policies on racism.

Awareness in the group was wide ranging: one man was an active trade unionist who saw racism as part of the divide-and-rule tactics practised in British society; one of the women said she felt very ignorant, and her daughter often accused her of making racist remarks; one of the younger white men had been attacked, unprovoked, by a group of black youths, his friend permanently injured. He was worried about violence from both sides and was trying to understand the motives. The other young white man was the first to acknowledge his own overt racism. He felt he had been brought up actively to dislike black people, and knew that he'd often been guilty of racist abuse. The one black man in the group had been the victim of such abuse and attacks ever since arriving in Britain and felt he needed every opportunity to talk with white people, to try to understand them.

By now it was clearer why members of the group had wanted to discuss the issue, and we had some basis for moving on. We had a general brainstorm around 'prejudice' and 'racism' and the group came up with a wide range of first thoughts: hatred, ignorance, fear, ethnic divisions, the National Front, trouble in Ireland, South Africa, problems with housing and employment, religion, conflict, violence, differences, discrimination. Then we noted some of *our prejudices*, for example towards the Scottish, other religions, women, leaflets in foreign languages, bad manners. We kept the list deliberately broad and therefore less controversial than one which a narrow focusing on racism might have produced. We could then conclude, after discussion, that 'prejudice' was a 'dislike based on ignorance' or 'thinking badly of others for no good reason'.

So we were all prejudiced in various ways, some of us by now acknowledging some form of *racial* prejudice in ourselves.

We then moved on to ask the question, 'How easy is it to generate prejudice?' We watched a short extract from the film *Eye of the Storm* as used in the video, *Black*. (This shows an experiment in an American infant school in the 1950s where a group of white children were persuaded to dislike each other on the basis of an arbitrary physical characteristic – the colour of their eyes.) The film had an immediate impact and we were able to discuss what makes people prejudiced.

Now we could move on to try to define 'racism'. We used a sheet from the Open University pack, 'Racism in the workplace and the community', discussing power, assumed superiority, discrimination, being racist in effect as well as intention.[3] There our first session ended.

This session lasted about one and a half hours, and set the scene for a further full day's work on the issue (some of it spent visiting schools and particular anti-racist projects in Sheffield) plus an extensive report-back on the third day.

What happened in this first session was more than could have resulted from either a 'liberal' notion of pooling ideas for the sake of it or a dogmatic insistence on accepting anti-racism as a principle. Rather, by taking it step by step, building up trust and using additional resources, the group came both to recognize the limits of their individual experiences and to see how, put together with others and set against further information, they could form the basis for improved understanding. This principle of starting from people's experiences is not new and has certainly been practised in adult education since the early 1970s (strengthened by the growth of oral history projects and local publishing, and reinforced and refined by the women's movement). What is new is these methods are now being used in the context of paid leave.

Please release me. . .

In one sense going on a course is 'taking a chance', as the writers said in the introduction to this chapter; but in another, there is not so much to lose – it's worktime, and the money will be the same at the end of the week. As a result, people come on Take Ten who would never otherwise decide to enrol in adult education in their 'own time' – perhaps because they would not have any time (particularly in the case of women with children) or because 'it's not what people like us do'. This particularly seems to apply to working-class men of all ages, who, in our experience, do not attend social and political classes of this kind in other adult-education programmes in large numbers. Release from work has opened up, for those who have been through Take Ten courses, a kind of education to which otherwise, we suspect, they would never have been attracted.

However, the argument for release of this kind is not just about making it possible for more working people to take up adult education. It is about *time* that has been won by the workers: it is now theirs in a way that it wasn't before. Framed by the worktime of the rest of the week, release can become 'quality time', uncluttered by all the time-devouring activities which fill up a working life. Obviously this time is always dependent on the continuing existence of work, (and can be a mere short break from 'tedium' – to get back to that piece of writing at the beginning). Take Ten does not break the link with work but makes it a collective issue; the courses bring people together from all departments, women and men, young and old, manual and non-manual and, with the stress on common purposes, makes release not only time away from usual work but also a release from simple individualism ('Rise with your class, not above it'). For many women, for instance, having the time to listen and be listened to, whilst learning about women's issues in a structured context, has meant a change in the way they feel about themselves, seeing their own experiences in a wider context. For men the effects are different but may be similarly far-reaching. Sometimes they have talked personally about themselves and their relationships, past and present, in a way which would be inconceivable in most other educational settings.

We have grasped these opportunities as best we can. On one of the more recent courses, for instance, a small men-only group looked at male violence, beginning to consider the links between images of male sexuality, fantasy and rape. The beginnings are, of course, small, but they are part of a wider politics which will have repercussions at home, in the community and at work.

And the future...

By the time this chapter appears in print, Take Ten will have been going for over four years. By that time almost 800 council workers will have been through the scheme. Some of them will have become stewards, some will be less likely to dismiss the union out of hand, and some will be taking up further educational opportunities. We hope by then Take Ten will be at least Take Twenty, and that there will be a range of follow-on opportunities for those who want them.[4]

That's being optimistic. We are also aware that our form of political education, as well as making the courses successful, may make them vulnerable. Any nonvocational PEL designed to enable workers to understand their situation and give them the confidence to change it will always face opposition from some quarters. Schemes like Take Ten rely for their continued existence on a certain far-sightedness from both management and the unions, for the impact of the courses may not be to either's immediate advantage. In Sheffield there is at present a strong political commitment to shielding the scheme from attack; but in other places – and at other times – that might not be so.

9
Second Chance to Learn (Liverpool)

Eileen Kelly and Judith Edwards

'Second Chance to Learn' is advertised as 'a course for working-class people who are concerned about the problems of Merseyside today'. It focuses on the part played by 'ordinary people' in shaping events past and present, and studies the social, economic and political forces which have influenced Merseyside's growth and decline. One of its most striking features is that it encourages and seeks to equip students to play a more active part in their communities and workplaces.

Second Chance draws together, for one day a week, a mixed group of women and men of different ages with different experiences, united by a shared desire to make sense of society and to assist in bringing change towards greater equality. The 60 students attending the course each year include a (decreasing) proportion of full-time workers who struggle against a variety of obstacles to obtain release from their work for one day each week. If employed people are to have the opportunity to learn alongside the unemployed, housewives and retired men and women, PEL is a necessity. Few of Second Chance's students have obtained it. Most have suffered. What follows is an account by two of us – both course tutors – of a research project we carried out in the summer term 1986 with a group of eight Second Chance students, to examine the experiences and difficulties faced by some of the full-time workers who have attended the course over the years.

The students working with us were all volunteers who were members of that year's course.[1] The research provided an opportunity to pursue in practice some of Second Chance's stated aims. The process of gathering the information became an important part of the project, actively engaging the students by drawing on their ideas, experiences and knowledge, building up their skills and linking this educational exercise to campaigning for change. We held meetings to discuss the aims and scope of the research and to agree on the steps that would have to be taken to collect the information required. Some students sifted through course records to identify which previous students had been in full-time work in past years. We devised two questionnaires: the first, a general one requiring a postal reply; the second, for use in a smaller number of interviews which were to be organized. Our goal was to discover which employers granted leave; what negotiations were undertaken; if paid leave was not achieved, what alternative arrangements were made; what problems were encountered; and why education mattered so much to those who came on the course.

In all, seventeen interviews were conducted, and the findings from these and the thirty-five postal replies were collated. The group analysed the responses and discussed general issues and observations. The main conclusions were then written up. Finally, all those involved read and wrote comments upon the final accounts. The two of us acted as editors in putting together what follows. In short, a fair amount of work was done by the research team on a voluntary basis. It was motivated by a genuine concern to assist in extending educational opportunities to other working-class adults and a belief that there should be more courses like Second Chance which aim to address current social and economic problems.

What is 'Second Chance'?

To put the results of our research in context, we need to make some points about the kind of course that Second Chance is, and particularly about its aims, curriculum and student membership.

The course sets out to:

1 provide community activists, trade unionists, and adults whose circumstances have isolated them from collective action but who are concerned about Merseyside, with the knowledge, skills and confidence they need in order to make a useful contribution to reversing Merseyside's decline;
2 open up educational and job opportunities to those whose formal education stopped short at sixteen or earlier;
3 enable students to fulfil themselves through education, to discover and develop their talents and equip them to carry on learning independently when they leave the course.

As well as examining the history of Liverpool and the causes and consequences of its decline, students learn how to study in a series of study skills workshops; they develop their talents to write creatively in the writers' workshops; and they analyse the media and learn how to write for and produce community newspapers. This highly rigorous course is supported by a tutorial system in which every student meets her/his tutor each week for an hour-long individual tutorial. Students are expected to read quite lengthy course notes each week at home and most also attempt to write essays, read additional materials and complete other course work.

Underpinning the course is the view that education is part of everyday life, feeding off and into real issues of concern – that it has a practical value informing action and involvement, and contributes not only on an individual level to personal enrichment but also on a collective level to social and political change. Almost all the students (who are aged 18 to 70-plus) left school at minimum school leaving age with no qualifications. For more than half, Second Chance is the first course they have ever attended since leaving school. Approximately 15–20 per cent are employed full time; 30–35 per cent are women at home caring for families (many also working part time), and an increasingly large proportion are unemployed. About one third of all students are 'activists' – men and women who are members of tenants' associations, trade unions, political parties or voluntary groups, and who are committed to trying to bring about changes and improvements. Most live in the inner city or on the large 'overspill' estates on the outskirts of Liverpool. About 500 have attended the course since 1976.

Initially established through funding from the Gulbenkian Foundation, Second Chance has since been financed from a variety of sources. From 1978 to 1987 it was funded by the Inner City Partnership Scheme, and jointly sponsored by the Workers' Educational Association and Liverpool University's Department of Continuing Education. In April 1987 it became part of Liverpool's City College of Further Education. Fuller accounts of the course have been written by Martin Yarnit (1980) and Judith Edwards (1986).[2]

PEL and Second Chance: who gets it and how

Over the last ten years there has been a sharp decline in the numbers of Second Chance students who are full-time workers. The proportion has dropped from 30–40 per cent (1977–80) to 15 per cent (1984–6). These workers have come from a varied field of employment: private industry, voluntary organizations, community services, local authorities, the NHS, public transport and MSC schemes. More than half have been employed to provide services for others (youth workers, houseparents, nurses, etc.). The proportion of workers employed by private industry has dropped noticeably. Second Chance students are more likely now to be employed by voluntary organizations such as neighbourhood councils.

In our research study, we found that less than a quarter of all workers have been paid whilst attending Second Chance. For some paid leave was achieved by stealth; the employer did not know, and other workers covered up their absence. Nearly all those who were granted paid leave by their employer were expected to catch up on their work on other days of the week. In fact, some of those who were *not* granted paid leave were expected to catch up their work, too, effectively donating a day's work to their employer! Almost all those employers who granted leave were in the voluntary agencies. There is only one known case of a worker in private industry being granted leave and it was his site agent (on a building site) who gave permission informally. Many workers have been granted leave without pay. All those who worked for local authorities, the transport service, the NHS and private companies fell into this category. All lost wages or found ways of minimizing these losses by working an extra day, using their holiday allowance or changing their shifts.

Overall, only five of our seventeen interviewees had achieved really satisfactory arrangements and it is interesting to note that two of these worked for a voluntary organization which has close links with Second Chance: one of the Second Chance tutors is a member of the organization's management committee. Two others worked for another voluntary organization whose chief officer was married to a Second Chance tutor, and one of these two remarked: 'Play-leadership, to be good, involves a lot of organization and preparation, so I still have the same amount of work to do in four days instead of five.' We have to conclude, therefore, that the chances of full-time workers obtaining satisfactory paid leave for education on Merseyside have always been extremely poor, are diminishing in the current economic climate, and are virtually nil unless they are employed by voluntary organizations closely linked to Second Chance.

When we explored how workers had gone about securing leave arrangements with their employers we discovered that trade unions had played little part. More than a third of our sample had approached their employer directly. A similar number did not attempt to negotiate paid leave and made instead informal arrangements with their colleagues. Only a quarter obtained help from their unions and most of these were themselves shop stewards.

A number of factors may help to explain why so few sought and obtained help from their union. In very small workplaces workers may have thought it unnecessary. Other workers may have felt so certain of refusal that they preferred to make informal arrangements rather than alert the employer about their intentions. Some workers expected (or even experienced) an unhelpful, negative response from their unions. It is not surprising that in a period of rundown on Merseyside the trade unions are fully stretched fighting closures and redundancies. Other issues may well seem irrelevant or even a diversion. The role of trade unions in Britain has been rather narrowly defined as that of representing members' interests in the workplace. Other issues, sometimes referred to as 'the social wage', have played little part in their negotiations and the time is hardly opportune to reverse this trend. Yet, as we shall see later, many workers believe that it is becoming increasingly important to establish the right to paid educational leave.

Problems Encountered by Full-time Workers

Whether they obtained paid leave or not, virtually every worker who has attended Second Chance to Learn over the past ten years has experienced numerous difficulties. In questionnaires and interviews these were graphically illustrated.

MONEY

Many Second Chance students sacrificed part of their wages in order to attend the course. A full day's wage meant a loss of more than £1,000 over the year to one worker, for example. Others lost bonus payments and similar benefits. On top of that, money had to be found for bus fares, books, stationery, educational visits and, sometimes, childcare. Even though the course is free, these hidden costs soon mount up. Some of the students who lost out financially felt guilty about the impact upon their families and, in a few cases, experienced resentment or hostility at home. Others tried to compensate by working overtime or unsocial hours, often resulting in ill health or strain.

TIME

Shortage of time presented numerous problems to full-time workers. Both men and women described the exhaustion they experienced as they tried to combine their jobs, their course work and their domestic responsibilities. Not surprisingly women suffered most, carrying – as they inevitably did – the responsibility for family and home. Some men talked of domestic strains created by their study. They had no time or energy left to do their normal household jobs such as house repairs, decorating, etc. Some described how their wives felt excluded by their new area of interest. One man explained it this way:

> You are at work all day. If you come home and start wanting to shut yourself off in a room to write all night (I usually fall asleep anyway) it's not surprising that your wife (who also works) just may start calling you ignorant, unfeeling, selfish, exploitative; 'You do have a child!', and she may have a point.

Several workers claimed that their attendance had been less regular because of work responsibilities. If a crisis occurs in a small community organization or if there is a major dispute going on in a big company, workers feel obliged to sacrifice their 'day off' to remain at work. It must be noted, though, that the attendance records of full-time workers overall compare favourably with those of other students on the course. Although some had been prevented from attending by work pressures and some had even had to leave as a direct result, others had made a supreme effort to attend and every year some of the full-time workers had the best attendance records of all. One man, for example, who swapped to permanent nights in order to attend, came on to Second Chance after a night's work, without sleep. There were several students who missed only one or two attendances over the whole year. When they have to make such sacrifices and overcome so many hurdles, many students seem even more determined to attend, provided that the course lives up to their expectations. The price they paid in tiredness and strain was high. Loss of sleep, arranging with colleagues to work unsocial hours in order to cover up their absence, working overtime to make up lost pay, working at the weekend, all led to exhaustion. One-third of the students we contacted felt disappointed that they had no energy left to keep up with homework and so had not benefited as much as they might otherwise have done:

> As I had to make up my time I had to work a six day week. This made it very difficult to keep up with homework and I started to suffer fatigue when attending Second Chance which made it difficult for me to concentrate and I became a little irritable with fellow students.

Each year about one third of all full-time workers gave up the struggle and left the course.

PROBLEMS AT WORK

More than half our students mentioned a variety of problems they experienced at work as a result of asking for, or taking, leave to attend Second Chance: 'The company didn't want to know if they weren't going to benefit. They were very negative.' A quarter experienced difficulties with their employers. None of these had been granted paid leave. They had all changed shifts, lost pay or worked extra hours. Yet their employers still appeared to assume that concessions had been made which warranted some special return. One found that his time-keeping and sickness came under special scrutiny and on one occasion, threatened disciplinary action was only averted when his union was called in to intervene. Others were expected to speed up their workrate to catch up. One was often involved in arguments over changed shifts. His employer accused him of interfering with the smooth running of the factory.

A shop steward (taking unpaid leave) who was ever-vigilant about manning levels described the difficulties he encountered:

> On my day off at Second Chance they would try to persuade my workmates to do a job with one man instead of two. This reduced the agreed safety levels. Most of my mates usually refused, so they were put on another job and a more acquiescent worker would agree to do it on the reduced level. When I took it up the next day the boss would say that he was covering for me. Eventually I went to senior management over it but it was never properly resolved. To be honest, not all the men were behind me because some saw the reduced manning levels as my fault, not the management's.

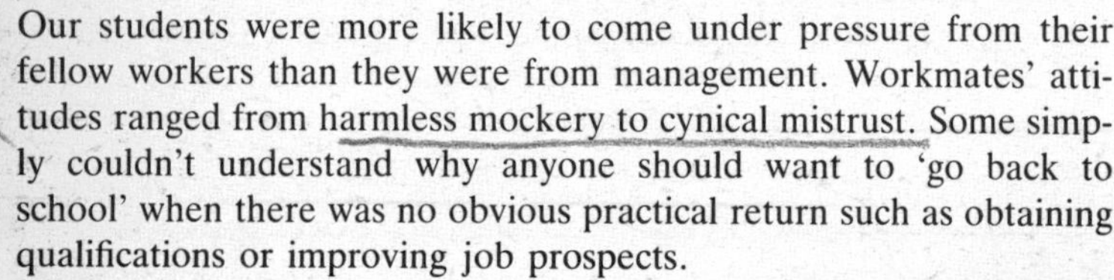

Our students were more likely to come under pressure from their fellow workers than they were from management. Workmates' attitudes ranged from harmless mockery to cynical mistrust. Some simply couldn't understand why anyone should want to 'go back to school' when there was no obvious practical return such as obtaining qualifications or improving job prospects.

Some assumed that the Second Chance students were taking a day off to do something else rather than actually attending the course. There were more serious problems than this, especially when the student was a shop steward. Some workers accused the student of attempting to gain special privileges, believing the day's leave represented the beginnings of a sell-out to management; that a steward who had been granted such a privilege would feel beholden to the management and, therefore, be less willing to represent them properly in workplace disputes. Students who reported such problems with their workmates commented that they had not encountered this opposition when they had been granted time off to attend trade union shop-stewards' courses. This was because their workmates could recognize that they would personally benefit if their steward was better equipped to negotiate with management on health and safety arrangements, etc. When stewards attended Second Chance, their workmates could not see that it would benefit *them*; yet many Second Chance students who were stewards explained how they were able to act more effectively as stewards because of their improved understanding and their increased ability and confidence to communicate and argue effectively, which they had gained from the course.

NO COVER

The resentment students experienced from workmates was undoubtedly fuelled by lack of cover for a worker's absence. No one we spoke to had succeeded in getting paid cover for their day at Second Chance, and a quarter said that their workmates were expected to cover for them without extra pay. Small wonder some felt angry. In their eyes, they were working harder to give cover to enable someone to go on a course for his or her own personal benefit. It was the other workers who paid the costs of PEL, not the employers.

Lack of proper cover throws into question what is meant by paid educational leave, because without cover the consequences are either exhaustion and strain for a worker who has to cope with a backlog of work during the remainder of the week, or anger from colleagues who feel personally resentful at their increased workloads and anxious about the opportunity afforded to management to erode staffing levels. If someone can be easily spared one day per week, this implies that fewer workers are really needed to do the job.

It was clear from our research that small firms and voluntary organizations could not easily spare a worker and could never afford to replace her or him. Someone had to suffer – worker, colleagues, customers/clients or management – and this will continue until proper government-backed and financed arrangements can be made.

WOMEN'S PARTICULAR DIFFICULTIES

All but one of our sample believed that women face additional problems both in securing leave and simultaneously coping with domestic responsibilities. Prevailing attitudes towards women's work and educational needs means that requests for PEL are not taken seriously by many employers or trade unions or, indeed, sometimes by women themselves. One woman student put it this way:

> Most people consider men as the breadwinner and accept that further education can improve his career or job prospects. A woman, on the other hand, works for 'pin money'. She wouldn't see the need for furthering her education to improve her job prospects.

The view that women's *real* place is in the home, and that paid work is simply to supplement the family income, acts as a permanent drag on women achieving equality as workers. Closer to home, many experience opposition and even downright hostility from their partners over their return to education. Accepted patterns of behaviour and family routines are threatened. This might mean that dinner is not on the table at the accustomed time or, much more seriously, that the women begin to challenge their accepted roles and question the distribution of work and responsibility in the home. Most of the women we talked to had experienced these difficulties:

> Before I came on Second Chance to Learn my husband used to help me in the house, do the dishes and so on (we both work full time and have four children). But since I've gone on the course he does much less than before. It's very noticeable. I know he doesn't like me doing it, and it seems as if he's determined to make it as hard for me as possible without actually saying I can't go.

Other women encountered resentment and sometimes hostility from neighbours, parents or friends:

> I felt as though the neighbours were talking about me. You know the sort of thing, 'Look at the state of her!' They thought I was snobby, too big for my boots, going back to school.

For some women it was their own conditioning, their own attitudes, which held them back:

> After years of being totally involved with rearing my children and keeping house as well as going out to work, I found it very difficult to allot time to myself. My husband and children have been very supportive. My worst enemy is myself. I still tend to leave study time until most of the chores are done, by which time I'm tired out.

Finally, it must be noted that several students said they experienced no problems coming on the course: three because their employer was supportive and understanding; others because they had supportive partners or few domestic responsibilities. They had enjoyed the stimulation of learning and so had been able to take in their stride the relatively minor inconvenience and readjustments. Several men compared their experience of Second Chance with that of attending trade union studies courses. One man made this comparison which reflects the views of several others and helps us understand why, despite hardships, workers carried on coming:

> On trade union shop-stewards courses we were paid. There was no work to do outside the classroom. It was a totally accepted practice so there was no opposition. Second Chance is much more demanding, it's much harder to attend, but it's personally more rewarding.

Why Second Chance to Learn?

The catalogue of problems outlined above demonstrates the lengths that workers will go to in order to pursue relevant education, even when it does not lead to any material gain such as qualifications or improved job prospects. Popular assumptions that working people are not interested in education, that they are apathetic about what is going on around them and interested only in their personal lives or material gains have all been challenged by the experience of workers attending Second Chance to Learn courses.

When they were asked to explain why Second Chance meant so much to them, what they had hoped to get from it and what they had gained, more than three-quarters of the students we talked to mentioned the importance of the course's content in influencing their decision to apply. They wanted to study national and local economic, social and political issues; to examine the way society is run and why, and to consider the position of the working class and to get involved in changing things:

> I had a feeling that I could do something more with my life. I felt that I had something to offer society and needed to channel it. I also like the course curriculum as I have a strong interest in and feeling for Liverpool and its unique problems.

> The course makes us aware of our own importance in society, so that we can take an active part in running our own futures and have confidence that we can. Knowledge has given us that confidence.

There was a keen interest in education rooted in the real world, based on information and debate:

> I became aware of my ignorance as to what was going on in the world. I realized how much I didn't know, and how much I did *want* to know.

> I wanted to stop moaning about the price of food and bus fares and be able to understand why they are rising and whether anything can be done about it.

Students wanted to develop particular skills in order to express themselves more confidently and fluently in both writing and speech. These practical skills are often neglected in both education and 'activist' circles yet they are vital if working-class people are to take greater control of their lives:

> You could say I was written off at school. Nobody bothered whether we did our work or not so long as we kept out of trouble. I left unable to put more than a couple of sentences down on paper. I can't tell you how much that has hurt me and held me back over the years. Now I'm writing pages and pages at a time. Something has been unlocked inside. I've got so much to say. It's like a dam bursting open, just because someone stopped and took the trouble to show me how to spell, where to put full stops, commas and things. The thing is I've been a big union activist for years, well known throughout Liverpool, and no one knew I couldn't write. It was easy to avoid things. But I can't begin to describe how different I feel inside now, just because I can write.

Many students talked about wanting to realize their potential and release intellectual energy which had been stifled by school and by boring, uncreative and undemanding work:

> I wanted to increase my understanding of the social and political environment which governs our lives, partly as I am a trade union-

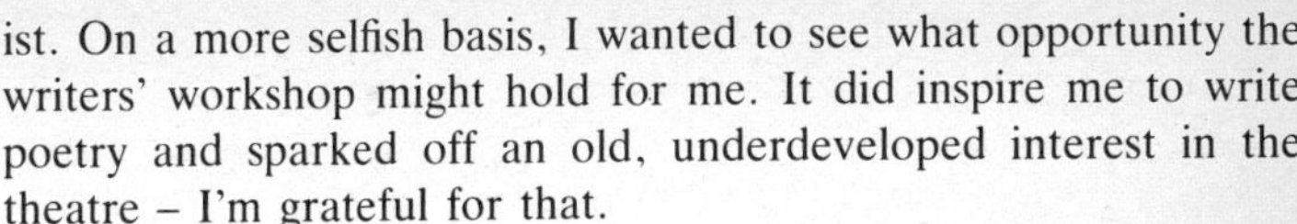

> ist. On a more selfish basis, I wanted to see what opportunity the writers' workshop might hold for me. It did inspire me to write poetry and sparked off an old, underdeveloped interest in the theatre – I'm grateful for that.

The course's relaxed, informal style based on exchange of ideas and information, and the absence of exams, attracted students yet, at the same time, they wanted the challenge of a course which made intellectual demands. More than half expressed the need for mental stimulation. They were 'driven crazy' by jobs which offered no opportunity for initiative, choice or even thought:

> I wanted an opportunity to do something different to factory work – it was soul destroying. I wanted an opportunity to break away.

Why paid educational leave?

> I've worked all my life (I'm in my fifties). I've done my bit for the community, for the country, for other people's businesses. I deserve something back.

> I believe people have a fundamental right to improve their school education. Management go on courses, workers should have the same privileges.

> Further education is very important today because of high unemployment – and it is even more important to have the chance before you become unemployed, as the depression which the unemployed usually suffer from becomes a barrier in itself when making the first steps towards education.

Comments like these capture the flavour of the statements made by Second Chance students as they argued for the rights of workers for leave to further their education. They pointed out that most working people have had a very limited education yet they have paid through their taxes and rates to support a system which has afforded far better opportunities to others. Once these better-educated adults begin their careers they are sent on further expensive management courses, or seconded to go on education courses, thus furthering their career prospects. The same chances should be available to all.

Students emphasized the way education improves the quality of life for an individual, who can enjoy a fuller, more meaningful, less stressful life:

> I believe education is a part of life, not a special activity for a minority. In a broad sense it should enable people to reach fuller potential. We've only got one life and the opportunity should exist to live it to the full. There should be less of a distinction between work and retirement and instead a more gradual transition – with a shorter working week and more time for education throughout our working lives.

Some students said that education can also enable people to take more control over their lives by analysing what is happening and recognizing the part they and others can play in the decision-making which affects them. When more people understand the causes of economic decline they can take action rather than passively accept its consequences. If in the end they fail and redundancies occur, they will, through their education, be more ready and willing to change and adapt themselves to new circumstances.

Many of the students we talked to, particularly those who are shop stewards, pointed out that employers are unlikely to believe it is advantageous to them to allow their workers to educate themselves and, therefore, the right to PEL will only be won, like every other statutory right that workers have won in the past, by a concentrated trade union campaign leading to parliamentary legislation. It is, therefore, with the unions that the argument must be won so that their full support can be enlisted; and it is becoming increasingly urgent. The few opportunities which once existed for PEL are dwindling rapidly. Most of those we talked to who had taken time off several years ago said they could not ask for it now; jobs are too scarce and workers are afraid to ask for special privileges. Yet, with ever-increasing unemployment, it has never been more important to work towards a system where regular leave for education can bridge the gap between work and early retirement and can provide personal fulfilment to workers threatened by redundancy and uncertainty.

10

150 Hours (Bologna, Italy)

Anna Brasolin and Sonia Villone
(translated by Jane Mace and Martin Yarnit)[1]

For those adults who have decided to return to the classroom, the academic year begins on 10 October. In the morning, over five hundred children occupy the buildings of Gandino middle school in the centre of Bologna. This year, in the afternoon, seventy-six adults are there: among them, workers, unemployed people, housewives and also conscripted soldiers. (In the nearby barracks, many of the soldiers, especially 19–20-year-olds from the south, have hardly had any schooling.)

The adults are divided into four courses. Two courses run from 3.15 p.m. to 6.45 p.m., and the other two from 5.15 p.m. to 8.45 p.m. Their needs are various. Nora, Franca, Eleonora and Maria Rosa are housewives, and they want to attend the earlier course in order that they can be back at home in time for the evening meal. Nevio, Antonio, Barbara and Giovanna (16–17-year-olds) are unemployed; or rather, they are seeking work for the first time. They, too, come in the afternoon – at least until they can find a job – so they can keep their evenings free. Rita, Enzo and Roberto, on the other hand, have jobs, and they are attending the course partly in work hours. For their categories of employment (commerce, transport and engineering), the national agreements include the right to study for those who lack the basic secondary school qualification. This means, in effect, that they can take 150 hours' release from work, without loss of pay, within this academic year, on the basis of attending a course which lasts at least 350 hours. Their course time, then, is almost equally divided between their own 'spare' time, and company 'work' time. For the engineering workers such as Roberto, and for textile workers, there is a better agreement. This allows them up to 250 hours a year for study. For these groups of workers, the relationship between their own time and worktime changes, and becomes ⅓ : ⅔.

More workers and fewer housewives and unemployed people attend the early evening courses. They tend to be working in places where there is no national agreement on paid release for education; this includes small businesses, shops, those working with craftsmen, and the self-employed. They will have left work at 5.00 p.m. and got home around 9.30 p.m., having worked for eight hours and then been on the course for a further three and a half.

Courses in the town centre have always had a smaller percentage of course members on paid release than those located in the factory areas. Today in Bologna, the average number of adult students on paid release is 20 per cent. In 1974, when the so-called '150 Hours' courses began, however, 90–100 per cent of course members had release. Since the 1970s, over a million adults have attended '150 Hours' courses. Most of them were employed in engineering, textiles, hospitals, local authorities, the chemical industry and public transport. In the late 1970s, other groups increasingly began to join the courses: unwaged adults, housewives and the unemployed, particularly, school leavers. There are now so many of these, together with service workers (in commerce, private transport), and craftsmen, that often, in a course group, they outnumber those on paid release from employment. The 16- and 17-year-olds, too, are growing in numbers on the '150 Hours' courses. The minimum age for enrolment is 16; selection procedures in the morning middle schools are becoming stricter, and school students who fail their year drop out, or maybe stay on a year or two, and then later enrol for the adult courses.

So, over the last ten years, the use of the '150 Hours' courses has changed. Three main trends have contributed to this change: the increase in the number of women; the lowering of the average age of the students; and the increase in the numbers of those who do not get paid release. The courses, however, are still called the '150 Hours'.

Not everybody knows how the course is organized until they start. They will have to attend four sessions a week, Monday to Thursday. Obviously there is no homework, so attendance at the classes is important. There will be nothing to pay, either for the course fees, for books (they can use the class library) or for course materials (supplied free). All they will have to buy will be pens and notebooks. Students who have children will have to find their own solutions – using grandparents or relatives – for the four afternoons a week. Unfortunately, husbands often cannot or will not help wives with childcare. Nora, Eleonora and Franca already know that they have no one to help out, and ask, diffidently, if they can bring their children with them. Neither the education system, run by the state, nor the local authority, nor the trade unions have reached any practical solution to this problem, such as crèche provision. (Even a crèche would not be simple: the children often span a wide age range.) The fact that, throughout the city, only a few cases surface publicly at the same time, allows the issue to be avoided. Yet how many women with children must there be who do not even try to enrol, knowing, as they do, that there is no provision made for childcare on the courses? Eleonora will end up by giving up the course after a few months. She has had to choose between her daughter and her own education.

'150 Hours' is organized or financed by two institutions:
The state *This provides premises, some of the teaching materials, and teaching and non-teaching staff. There has always been a tendency to regard the courses as temporary, so each year, since 1974, they have had to be renegotiated. Adult education in general, indeed, has never had any real priority, nor even adequate facilities. It's worth recalling that in 1974 the trade unions had estimated that 70 per cent of Italian workers had not completed their basic secondary schooling.*
Local authorities *They provide (or should provide) the funds for adult education, run by the state or local authorities themselves. In the early years, Bologna Council and the Emilia Romagna Regional Authority (under a joint Communist/Socialist administration) were in the vanguard of the '150 Hours' scheme; Bologna Council, in employing its own teachers for the courses, and the Regional Authority, in providing finance. Local authorities, too, were among the first employers to grant release for the '150 hours' courses. The new regulations which required a middle school certificate qualification for all new employees in local government may well have been a stimulus: as employers, they had a certain responsibility to those among their existing employees who did not have this qualification. Now, local authorities have lost their early impetus, and they too*

have to be persuaded and urged on each year by the union organizations. Emilia Romagna Regional Authority, for instance, has no budget in 1986 for basic adult education, even if PEL is still given to its employees. Local authorities now are much more interested in vocational training: an area which attracts much greater funding, and for which employees are now gaining release.

In short, if the unions were to drop their commitment to the middle-school courses for adults, there is no doubt they would soon close. As it is, every year, nearly 100,000 people nationally enrol on these '150 Hours' courses. There are some 4,900 courses; fewer than some years ago (the peak was in 1981 with 5,800 courses; from then on, there has been a decline, particularly in the small towns). In Bologna, since 1975, the Centro Operativo Unitario (COU) has had its own '150 Hours' office. It is the one organization which brings together the three union federations (CGIL, CISL and UIL), and which, even in recent moments of crisis between these three bodies, still survives. It organizes the courses (publicity, enrolments, information for new students), monitors their progress (by periodic meetings with the teachers), negotiates annually with the education authority the number of courses in the town and the region, their location, the number of teachers, and obtains the funding for materials and publicity from the Region. COU has now extended its activities to vocational training and to research on the labour market.

At the beginning of the course, the tutors ask the students to discuss their educational experience. Asked, 'Why have you returned to study?' just two of the students reply: 'To improve my education', or 'Because I have often regretted not having completed my compulsory schooling'. They are Maria Rosa, a 50-year-old housewife, and Vincenzo, a bricklayer, aged 55. They are the oldest in the group. Their age is, it seems to us, an important explanation for these responses. The other nineteen course members each give the same reply: 'Because the certificate would be useful to me'. Some add other comments – such as the chance it would give to meet other people; and it's surprising that this last reply comes from the four youngest students, girls and boys of 16 or 17 years old. Perhaps it's sad; but we shall see later that they have particular personal and family situations.

So why is it that 19 out of 21 people (and in the other three

Gandino school courses we found a 90 per cent or more response of this kind) say that their aim in joining this course is to gain the school-leaving certificate? The fact is that for the last ten years or more, in Italy, officially, this certificate is required for any job in public service: not only for those working in office jobs, but also for cleaners, porters and caretakers. Since 1980 anyone who wanted to get a licence to open their own shop had to have the certificate; and since 1984 it has been required for anyone wanting to trade. What has happened is that the middle-school certificate has replaced the elementary (or primary school) certificate as the minimum qualification for a whole range of occupations.

Eight of the course members have had, in the past, some kind of middle-school education – mainly up to the second year, but some had also reached the third, before failing the exam, which led to a 'voluntary' dropout from school altogether. Thirteen others, by contrast, left after the fifth year of primary school: of these, eight come from southern Italy, where people have less schooling.

There are nine southerners on this course, and they include, not surprisingly, five of the six soldiers. In Italy military service always takes place far from home. This time, at least, it could mean an educational opportunity, and at least, it's worth a try. As it turns out, the problems of fitting in the course sessions with barrack duties will force five of the six soldiers to give up the course; or at least, to attend so irregularly that they cannot keep up with the coursework. Southerners are disadvantaged. In general, they have least education and most difficulty in keeping up with the course; and a lot of them give it up before the end. On the other hand, at least in the classroom, there is no sign of any racism or prejudice towards them. There are other young people as well as the soldiers. Some of them have enrolled on the advice of a social worker, who is giving support at a tricky point in their lives. The course, in these cases, is used as a chance for social rehabilitation, or to help them get the qualification so vital for them to get a job – or, simply, to arouse the young person's interest, as in Antonio's case. He's serving a sentence from the juvenile court. There are courses inside the prison, but the social worker has arranged for him to attend one outside. After four months, Antonio is lucky enough to get a job in a workshop, but it's far from the school, and he has to work till 6.00 p.m. So, with regret, he leaves the course.

Francesco is a drug addict, living in poor conditions with three of his family in a tiny flat. He talks about his problems and about drugs, and through the course he finds one possible way out: he makes contact with a community drug project and is accepted; but this means he has to move to another district and so he, too, has to give up '150 Hours'. Gabriele, on the other hand, who is 27, stays to the end of the course. He is already a member of a therapeutic community, is having treatment for his addiction, but never talks about it. A community worker comes with him every day to the school and picks him up afterwards, for the whole course. Barbara and Giovanna are both 16. Barbara has terrible family problems which force her to leave home; she has a social worker, and moves into various kinds of girls' hostels, but each time manages to get herself thrown out. After some months of spasmodic attendance, she vanishes without trace. Later, we find out she has become pregnant and has been thrown out of the last hostel, run by nuns. Giovanna is supported by her mother, who worries about the bad crowd in which she has got mixed up; but Giovanna eventually gets free of them, attends the whole course, and even passes the exam.

Then there is Luisa, who, at 27, already has three children, is separated from her husband, and lives, with the children, in a young mothers' hostel run by nuns. She wants to get a job and somewhere to live. For Eleonora, the course is just what she wants – if only her husband would help her with her daughter. Instead, she will have to drop out. Nora's interest in the course, which she only expresses indirectly, is to stop feeling inferior to her husband, who has more education than she does.

Often, then, within these courses, all the current social ills of society are represented by those who attend, old or young. Though living in the midst of others, many of them are very isolated. It's important, though, to note the particular environment of Gandino middle school. It is near the psychiatric hospital, the juvenile prison and a therapeutic drug project; so it is the natural place to which 'cases' get sent. At the same time, it's a long way from the factories. In the '150 Hours' courses further out from the town centre there is a very different course membership (as in most Italian towns); most students are workers (many with PEL) and housewives.

Since the early 1970s, there have been major changes in the aims of the '150 Hours' courses. At that time, the trade unions looked to these courses to achieve two very grand objectives:

1 to provide workers with the tools to understand and to change the organization of work within their own factory, as a first step to a more general and active involvement with the wider society;

2 *to develop, too, a critique for change within the system of education in which the children of '150 Hours' student-workers were even now involved. School was seen to be a powerful system of selection, discriminating by class and academic achievement, with methods, syllabuses and text-books which were out of date and often anti-democratic.*

So the unions were adopting objectives which aimed at the collective growth of workers. They wanted them to gain greater control in the society as a whole; they also wanted the '150 Hours' courses to meet individual needs for basic skills and increased understanding. Today, it is true to say that the '150 Hours' middle-school courses have only achieved this last objective, that of offering personal 'improvement'. The failure to achieve the more general objectives has to do with the fact that they were set too high for workers with little schooling, that seven months on a course was not long enough, and that the unions were not able to work out the best way to achieve them anyway.

The general aims remain, politically speaking, valid, and the adult courses could be the best place for them to be achieved; but middle-school courses probably can only be a first step towards them.

How did these adults find out about the courses? One of the best forms of publicity today is 'word of mouth'. Knowing people who have been on a course, or who know others who have, and who talk about their experiences, can awaken curiosity and give encouragement. (In the course we are describing, Nevio is a neat example of this. Two years ago, his mother attended a '150 Hours' course. This happened for Giovanna, too.) The second kind of publicity and recruitment which has been most successful is the kind that is aimed at everyone and anyone: posters on buses or in the streets, and so on. In short, publicity ranges from the informal and personal (friends, family, acquaintances) to the most general and public. Perhaps this is an indication of how the '150 Hours' courses have become genuinely open to all.

In Bologna, it is the trade unions, through COU, who, each year, organize the publicity campaign – with leaflets, posters, and letters delivered to those people who have not got the middle-school certificate. Normally the costs are met by the region. The state, on the other hand, just collects the enrolments for the courses through the schools.

> *'150 Hours' courses have been running now for twelve years in Bologna and in all the major towns in Italy. The best means of publicity, in the early years, was the trades unions; precisely because it was the unions, through the shop stewards, who collected the applications and negotiated in the workplace the practical arrangements for paid release. (Only 2 per cent of the workforce could be on release at any one time in a given workplace.) Gradually, then, COU, the '150 Hours' office, has become, in Bologna, a referral point for the unemployed, for women at home, and for non-industrial workers. Its work includes the villages in the whole Bologna province.*

The first part of the course year is always hard. People have to get to know each other, and there are difficulties to get over. The course members find themselves back on child-sized benches, and surrounded by drawings, graphs and posters made by middle-school children. Even the youngest members of the class, who like to appear confident, can't quite block out the bad associations of an environment which, only a few years (and, for some, just a few months) ago, they had left behind them. Nevio, aged 17, is the first to put this unease into words, in one of the earliest discussions. He asks not to be judged and labelled on the basis of his character and behaviour. Others will need more time to rationalize and express their fears and anxieties about returning to school. Later on in the year, they will succeed, once they have settled down. Maria Rosa, for example, will say, 'Now that I have got used to things I would like to stay for another year'. Vincenzo, who gets up every morning at five, always takes part in all the work. He wants to understand and learn; and the day he tells us he would never have imagined that school work could be so lovely and enjoyable, his eyes shine.

Discussion time in the class, with the exchange of ideas and experience, is important, and is a regular feature of the course. It provides a valuable opportunity for thinking about people's individual problems, for listening to each other's opinions and, sometimes, for disagreeing. For the teachers, too, it can be the best time to get a sense of the feeling of the group towards their learning, and to discover their interests and their needs, whether directly or, more often, indirectly expressed.

The job is not going to be easy: that's clear from the start. The group is very mixed, and the dynamics which are developing within it may end up undermining not only the teaching, but the very possibility of a common sense of purpose. The struggle to achieve a certain balance cannot be won in a few weeks, and it will continue throughout the course. The teachers have to take account of students' personal and family situations, which, as we've seen, are difficult. It's for this reason, for example, that they have had to organize the work in small units in order to keep the interest of the group. The older ones find it hardest to accept and understand the restless and impatient behaviour of the younger. For their part, the younger students, who have never acquired the habit of study, want none the less to be treated as adults. It will take a whole year for both sides to see that they *can* work together, not because anyone is forcing them to do it, but because they have something in common that they all want to achieve. The course year, anyway, is too short fully to work out these learning and socialization processes. It is, above all, an opportunity; and, perhaps, for some, a stimulus to go on to further education.

What is the content of the courses? and how are they organized? There is an attempt to invite the students to work out, with the teachers, what topics they would like to cover, and how; but it is soon clear that it is not enough simply for the teachers to put questions to the students and expect clear answers. For the most part, their interests are still only vague – but they are also, at the same time, wide-ranging. The main thing students express, at least at the beginning, is a sense of curiosity and expectation. This is what Roberto, the only engineering worker on the course, writes in his first essay: 'What do I expect? The chance to improve myself. At least it will be one more new experience – and, hopefully, a good one!' The teachers try, on the one hand, to exploit this sense of curiosity and, on the other, to enable the students to work out from their own accounts of their histories the issues which they want to look at in more depth. The aim is for students to become more conscious of their own experience, to be capable of communicating it and looking at it with other people and, in the end, to relate it to a more general understanding of the world.

The curriculum for the '150 Hours' courses in the middle school is laid down by the Ministry of Education (Ministro della Pubblica Istruzione), and there are fewer subjects than in the middle-school syllabus itself. There are three teachers for each course: one for Italian and history, one for mathematics and science, and one for the foreign language. Particularly in Bologna, for some years the foreign language element has become integrated in a broader programme of language education (Italian), with teaching aims, content and methods agreed among all the foreign language teachers and carried out in collaboration with their colleagues teaching Italian and history.

As for the content of each subject, there have been a number of changes since the early years of the '150 Hours' scheme, when everything was related to the world of work, and in particular to that of the factory. Today more time is given to current social problems which relate to the needs and demands of the new student body. In the Bologna courses, these are some of the subjects most frequently dealt with: health, nutrition, sexual relations, family relations, drug addiction, energy, pollution, elements of economy and political education (such as the powers of the state, the institutions, the Republican Constitution, and the role of the local authorities). These last issues, particularly, can provide good starting points for a rapid review of the phases of Italian history; but the choice of content is extremely flexible. Topics are developed according to the interests and curiosity shown by the students at various stages of the course. The debate as to the link between skills and content is still open, and in recent years has revived; whether, that is, it is more useful to concentrate on mainly technical exercises, or whether to give priority to substantive subject matter, as a means to enrich individual skills in comprehension, communication and active participation.

This is how, for example, the class carried out a project on nutrition. The teacher leads a discussion in which everybody speaks about their own habits and experiences. Alessandro, in military service, complains about the barracks canteen: 'second-rate food, too much fried stuff, and oil that's been used over and over again'. Rita makes everyone's mouth water with her descriptions of the menu at the restaurant where she works; but then she tells how, having to work without a break from 7.00 a.m. to 3.30 p.m., she does not get to eat herself until mid-afternoon. Her enormous sandwiches in the break between classes become proverbial! Giovanna is a fan of the latest 'fast-food' place to open in the town centre, and rattles off a list of English terms she has just learned; but Nora and Vincenzo won't be persuaded, and declare themselves pasta-lovers. Nevio claims that he can't be bothered with the fuss about meals; a sandwich gulped down in front of the television 'so as not to waste time', and he is off out with his friends. The discussion grows heated; everyone has something to say; the first questions and tentative replies begin to emerge. Some of them advance theories, often fragmentary ones which, once they have been written up by the teacher, help to broaden and deepen the various topics (for example, the changes imposed by work, the different role of the woman in the family, the spread of diets, the influence of Anglo-Saxon countries, etc.). Prejudices and commonplaces abound. The teacher, by the end, has to collect and organize the main points of the discussion on the black-board. It is a first stage in learning about taking notes. Later, texts, extracts and articles will be brought in, arranged according to reading difficulty, to take some of the problems further, to challenge prejudices and to focus more attention on social problems. (For example, in this subject area, the scientific aspects of food, the protection of consumer interests, product labels and their ingredients, how goods are produced and consumed, and the relevant legislation.) At this stage there will be exercises to gain a grasp of the written text, to begin to take notes from it, and, with the help of a teacher, to collect and use the appropriate vocabulary.

The teaching plan for the Bologna '150 Hours' middle-school courses follows a number of stages. These are:

1 *discussion and problem posing;*
2 *collection of documents and their interpretation (group or individual work, depending on the activities);*
3 *analytical work (using 'chalk and talk', written essays, and oral reports).*

The materials used on the courses are:

1 *'150 Hours' course library books, available in every school;*
2 *worksheets, tables of statistics and social studies;*
3 *interviews and visits by specialists;*
4 *visits out (to museums, meetings, etc.);*
5 *audio-visual aids, when these are available in the school.*

The course planning is left to the teachers, who meet weekly, either on a subject basis or as colleagues who work in the same school. In these meetings they discuss curriculum, methods and problems, and work on the preparation of materials such as worksheets and tables, etc.

In Italy, there is no specific training for the kind of work which '150 Hours' teachers have to do. (The same qualifications are required whether they are teaching children or adults.) Nor is there any developed theoretical framework in which to address the problems of adult education. The practical experience is therefore of crucial importance, and exchanges between teachers themselves are organized in the form of district seminars. These offer, too, at least a minimal training for new teachers (and there are some every year).

This way of organizing the work poses problems. The students often have very clear and traditional ideas about teaching, based on what they remember (albeit negatively) of school – for them the only point of reference. Roberto, one of the few to develop his own reading and cultural interests, cannot understand the value of group-work, and is concerned about wasting time, which could otherwise be taken up with useful exam preparation. The others also tend to focus their work towards the final exam. It is important to demystify it, at the same time showing other ways of assessing their progress and attainments. Maria Rosa, who is the class representative, frequently complains in the meetings with the teachers about 'the lack of time given to grammar and arithmetic'. She expresses a need common to many of her colleagues who would like to overcome their own lack of basic skills and who see grammar and arithmetic as providing the solution to their problems. Already in the first written essays, phrases like these appear: 'Going on training courses, I realized that compared to others, my Italian was almost at rock bottom' (Vincenzo); 'I would like to achieve something that I have never learned: to be able to express myself better when I am talking with my friends' (Enzo).

Many of them, besides, were expecting a kind of traditional lesson, in which learning would happen simply by listening to the teachers' explanations. The teachers, for their part, must not undervalue these opinions and needs; but, little by little, they will try to guide the students towards new methods and learning possibilities. Roberto and others like him will come to understand the value of groupwork, once he has experienced it, and seen the concrete results, even at a personal level. However, a lot of difficulties persist and, when at the end of the year it is suggested that there should be a joint group project on the issue of energy with the other classes in

Gandino school, there is strong resistance. To the teachers, it would provide a stimulus at a point in the course when a certain tiredness is setting in; but a lot of the students do not welcome the idea of working with people from other classes whom they only know from meeting them at break times or during socials. The problem is never completely resolved: 'In the group some people tend to do nothing, and to rely on the others' (Nora); 'It's hard to agree on how to work together when there are so many different ideas' (Luisa).

All in all, apart from some good results from the teaching point of view, the majority of the students retain a negative view of group-work carried out with students from other courses in the school.

The exam for the middle-school certificate is obligatory. It is taken at the end of the year (in early June) according to a timetable set down by the school authorities, with the course tutors themselves presiding, together with an external adjudicator. Students are graded, however, not just by the final exam, but also on a continuous assessment of all their course work. This takes account of the level at which they began, their attendance record and their class participation. Only if the last two have been judged inadequate is a student prevented from taking the exam. Effectively, then, all the students who take the exam will pass it. This is not true for middle-school kids.

The assessment of the whole year is not, as in the morning school, carried out by giving marks to the work. Instead, in each subject, there are regular reviews, with the aim of offering students a chance to reflect on their work, as well as to keep a record of their individual progress throughout the year.

The diploma given by the '150 Hours' middle-school courses to those who sit the final exam is exactly the same as the one which in Italy is awarded normally at the age of 14. It therefore has the same value, even if the courses are different in terms of planning, duration, content, methods and exam.

How do the students become involved in their own learning? The job of the teachers is to create the need for information through assignments, and to encourage students, through activities and discussion, to play an active role in deciding what is studied and in formulating problems. The teacher's role, then, is the role of *animateur*. Her or his own contribution becomes a response to the expressed needs of the students in the context of their activity. At the end of the year, a lot of the students will speak of how much they have gained from this way of working: 'You're more involved; you pay more attention' (Nora); 'You work harder' (Luisa); 'You learn more' (Franca); 'This way, I remember things better' (Giovanna); 'I find it easier to concentrate' (Gabriele).

The students also say that it has required hard work and considerable personal effort. The tutors' explanations are seen by some of the students as something which is necessary, but difficult to follow with the right concentration, and hard to remember. For others, on the other hand, these are crucial moments: 'I prefer to have things explained to me, so that I can then ask questions' (Enzo); 'I think I understand better when the teachers explain' (Vincenzo); and Nevio admits with honesty, 'When I have to do the work myself (even when I know that this is the best way of remembering things) I find I do it grudgingly.'

On the whole, however, the younger students tend to get involved when there is work they have to do. Most of them have enough study skills to avoid too much difficulty. The aim is to guide them through a series of stimulating activities which do not oversimplify things, to a more thorough approach to issues.

Apart from the challenge of such a range of interests and ages, the teachers also have to take account of an extremely wide range of ability. Next to young people who have only just left school are adults who are returning to study, having not put pen to paper for years. Some of them have developed interests which have led them to reading (Roberto sees himself as self-taught and Vincenzo has been on various training courses). Very few of them read a daily paper. Some cannot read or write at all. This is the case for Rita; she has enrolled for the second time on a '150 Hours' course, and she tells us – somewhat aggressively – that last year she had to give it up because she did not understand anything that they were doing on the course. With individual work and a lot of patience, she is beginning to build for herself a set of ideas built on her own personal home and work experiences. Rita will not solve all her problems, but the small results achieved so far will enable her to take an active part in the class and to shed much of her aggressiveness.

Given the problems in the class, and the students' own desire to improve their communication skills, language education is central to all the subjects. The teachers have developed a set of materials which is adaptable to a variety of levels, and has a variety of uses. For Rita, for example, this means learning to describe briefly and simply her own experience. Roberto and Vincenzo, on the other hand, have learned to better organize their ideas and concepts in written and oral form; and they know how to recognize the structure and argument within an article or text. In general, everyone has gained, through the course, a greater understanding of communication; a more considered attitude to reading, language use and the vocabulary, and thus a greater confidence in themselves.

The course is finished, but only 12 of the 21 original students have managed to complete it. This is typical of most of the '150 Hours' courses, given that attendance for four afternoons a week, for nearly eight months, is fairly demanding. Perhaps some of the students who left the course this year will return to it in the future; and that's what we hope. What about the others? Do they see this learning experience just as a break in their lives, or as a new departure? Recently, in all the courses, the teachers have often been asked about other possible courses for adults. This is a sign that the main objective of the '150 Hours', to begin a process of learning, is often achieved. The problem is that there is still no well organized, coherent system of education for adults, with clear opportunities for study, linked to each other with the possibility of moving from one to another. There is, in short, no educational route which one could embark on through various points of entry.

Institutionally, it is the Regional Authorities who should be developing plans of this kind, but they have only had their new powers for a short time, and they still have to develop the policy and legislation. In Italy, higher education for adults does not exist. The unions have experimented in Bologna and Milan for example, with a two-year high-school course, as a follow-up to the middle-school certificate. There have also been the single-issue courses (*corsi monografici*) run in collaboration with local authorities or the university. Finally, the introduction of new technology into the workplace has given a new impetus for appropriate courses, using the '150 Hours' release system, but for vocational education. Overall, however, what is lacking is a trade union strategy for adult education. That would mean taking account of one element, which twelve years ago the unions underestimated: namely, the fact that, since many workers had had little schooling and lacked the basic skills (which alone can ensure active and independent understanding and communication), there is a major problem in dealing with issues and arguments in any effective way. There are already signs of large numbers of people dropping out of vocational training courses for this reason;

and it is this, too, which prevented the original objectives of the '150 Hours' courses suggested by the unions in the seventies from being realized.

Adult education in Italy needs rethinking. There needs to be planning based on an evaluation of the '150 Hours', and, above all, it needs to be organized in such a way that all adults can find their own space within it.

Part III
Making PEL a reality

11

Groundwork and ground rules

Michael Cunningham

In our book, we tell stories (some successful, some not) of working people who have struggled to acquire education or training during their normal working hours. You'd expect some of the best advocates to be those very working people who happen to be employed in further and higher education. Sadly, this is not true.

My experience since 1979, as a NUPE full-time official responsible for members employed in universities and polytechnics in London, has taught me many things. One is that, to put it mildly, manual workers have a jaundiced view of the very system itself. Their views of academic staff are not unique: they are very well paid, they work very few hours, they are arrogant and they are always complaining about how dirty their classrooms are. The trouble is that manual staff think the same, by and large, about students as well: the students *also* complain about the standard of food, they drink too much alcohol, vomit all over newly-washed floors, have fights, are abusive and patronizing to staff, and generally lead lives that are at several removes from acceptable moral codes. Of course, all manual workers make exceptions, but their *overall* view is a critical, negative one – not a good start when we are trying to introduce PEL.

It has been part of my job to facilitate some of the early PEL initiatives described in this book, and I have asked many manual workers if they would consider going on and availing themselves of the educational facilities that they themselves service; some of their answers could not be printed here – for the reasons just given – other answers were less vituperative, but of no less concern; they were along the lines of 'it is not for the likes of us'. I was not so surprised by these responses – after all, I was their full-time official and I knew them at least reasonably well; what was more disturbing was that they replied almost identically when I asked them what they would think if their *children* displayed enthusiasm for such education!

Why should this be? After all, it is 'well known' that diplomas and degrees (as well as O and A levels and CSEs) constitute a substantial advantage in the jobs market. Alas, our constituents are unimpressed: they will eschew 'educational advantage' particularly if it means people 'losing their roots'.

This disaffection towards education is not unrelated to a more quantifiable disregard that our society has for manual workers: universities, polytechnics and the like continue to offer low pay (just over £2 an hour to cleaners and kitchen staff, for example), term-time-only contracts, cuts in hours, insecurity of tenure, and decreasing staffing levels (accompanied by *in*creasing work loads). Small wonder that workers feel less than committed to education.

I have also come to know that the commitment of these staff to their jobs displays a fervour and keenness that are not all that often matched by more 'skilled' colleagues, such as academics: they *know* how to get floors gleaming, they *know* how to produce attractive, nutritious food; they *want* to do all these things and more – but they are not given adequate facilities to do so. Many are the domestics who befriend individual students, listen to their worries and see them through their crises (something that the academics, administrators, welfare officers – even the Students Union – have been unable (or unwilling) to diagnose and deal with). Yet, these are the workers who are regularly ignored or abused by the generality of students and other staff, and who work under degrading conditions of employment. Add this picture of disrespect to the myriad hurdles vividly described elsewhere in this book (the obstacle races organized by trade unions and work supervisors, domestic demands and responsibilities), and it is scarcely surprising that working people are not beating a path to the door of adult education classes.

As a trade union official, I have had no opportunity to amend a long-held view that industrial and social struggle is basically down to 'them' and 'us'. I suppose what has become clearer to me at least is that you cannot easily predict the views of the *individuals* in the two camps. It is sadly obvious that some leading, influential trade union members are resolutely opposed to certain progressive moves (e.g. proposals to seek PEL rights); it is comforting tc know that some people occupying quite senior management and personnel positions are overtly sympathetic to trade union claims for PEL – that is, if the unions get round to putting the claims in (some of the most dramatic PEL initiatives – predominantly for job-related training, it is true –

have been employer-inspired and employer-led). Such goodwill needs to be exploited. It is also becoming increasingly clear that there are other senior management/personnel people around whose consciences need massaging, *and* who need to be approached by the trade union(s) *with a package*.

However, all the goody management people in the world – and even all the goody trade union people — will not make much of an impact if we haven't carefully prepared the ground. I am talking here of *outreach work*, to be done by local union activists and adult educationists *working in concert*.

Crude questioning (like the questions I have written about in the first few paragraphs of this chapter) will produce crude answers: interesting, informative, but we're not going to be able to change the world with them. The potential students need to be sought out gently and sympathetically, their needs and their wishes for training/education elicited and seriously listened to (no matter how impracticable they may appear). I fear I may never forget a (very well-meaning) branch secretary marching into a meeting of several dozen women domestics and, without any preamble, asked if any of 'you ladies' would like some 'lessons in reading and writing'. The man was almost blasted out of the room by the rightly outraged members, but he never understood why. That was in 1982; four years on, there were still no basic education courses at that workplace.

It is also important that the people who do this essential work must be seen and felt *not* to be in the pocket of management; conversely, it must be clear from the outset that they *are* working in close collaboration with the union.

It is surely worse than useless for such courses to be put on by management (even by management and union jointly) without the slightest consultation with the students themselves. This is an example of the top-down syndrome at its worst. The courses are for the students, and not for well-meaning administrators (and union branch officers). The potential students need their own time and space to discuss what *they* would like out of it, to make their own demands. They have had little enough voice in the past; it is now time to give it to them.

There are countless components to a good PEL scheme, and many would eloquently (and justifiably) lay claim to theirs being of fundamental importance. I will only say that a course that lacks carefully planned and *effective* outreach work of the type I have just outlined runs the serious risk of being paternalistic and relatively ineffective. It constitutes a very substantial 'on-cost', and management may require some persuading about it: Mary Wolfe's chapter (particularly pp. 98–100), throws useful light on this subject. For the outreach work (and ultimately the course), then, to go well, there needs to have been some good *groundwork* done with the union(s) and the management. First, the union: perhaps the most impressive evidence to emerge from our work on this book is to be found in the post-course survey done by the Second Chance workers (chapter 9) into the reasons why their students had opted to go back to study:

1 an examination of local and national, social and political pressures;
2 a look at how society runs;
3 the position of the working class;
4 writing and speaking skills – and the confidence to use them!;
5 mental stimulation.

An impressive list! And *conclusive* evidence, I believe, for asking the *students first* what they want to learn about, rather than serving up a *fait accompli*. Not only do basic education organizers have to do their outreach work; trade unions may have to start acquiring those skills as well!

Learning about the organization of one's job and about the employer's set-up is also an attraction: certainly my experience of running shop-stewards' courses tells me that it is a 'must' for them; why not membership training as well? The ability to speak up for oneself is also a good 'seller': again, it is an automatic component on shop-stewards' and safety-representatives' courses, so there can be little opposition to it being part of a PEL course. (A trade union branch might even suffer a brief access of enlightened self-interest and dream of acquiring one or two new activists or shop stewards out of the PEL exercise!)

It would be foolish to allow anyone to imagine that all these ideas will find universal popularity: in particular, the suggestion that some of the members ('They never come to meetings, you know! We have to do everything for them!') might start 'speaking up for themselves' could well be construed – and perhaps rightly – as a threat or challenge to long-established power-bases. Jane Mace's chapter on women (pp. 27–9) gives a full flavour of this kind of development: it has to be treated with the utmost diplomacy and tact, and experience shows that extensive lobbying prior to the meeting can pay dividends. In this context, modesty does not forbid me from saying that a well-timed word with the full-time official *can* work wonders in such situations: the full-timer is a sort of curator of the union's policies and is under much more of an obligation to abide by them – and s/he may well be quite sympathetic! (Incidentally, *never* venture into *any* PEL initiative *without* the full knowledge of the full-timer!)

Sometimes, employers/management can be pretty silly and play right into your hands. I remember the time when a particularly daft comment certainly hastened the extension of PEL: the trade union side had made a very mild request for more money to be set aside for manual-worker non-job-related training, and an extremely distinguished and senior member of one of Britain's leading universities said that it was quite unthinkable unless it could be shown that it would benefit the university! His unguarded pomposity produced such an outrage amongst the members that the employers were obliged to make a few more concessions much earlier than they had intended.

On a more mundane level, it should be remembered that the conservativeness of unions can be soothed by the mention of *precedents*: a branch might easily consider the idea of PEL for adult education as a bit 'fancy' or 'modern', but it may feel happier about moving into such experimental areas if you can talk about successful initiatives elsewhere – and this book has plenty of examples of that! This unease about paid time off work to follow a course appears to be paradoxical, because there are many thousands of people who go on shop-stewards' courses, apprenticeship courses and the like every year; however, as Martin Yarnit has shown in chapters 1 and 3, the beneficiaries tend to be male and white and able-bodied, and find it easier to leave their domestic responsibilities and come to meetings, thus appearing more experienced.

So much for the groundwork on the union. If the union has adopted a clear position supporting a claim for PEL, we now need to do some groundwork on the employer/management. First of all, we might need to draw a distinction between 'employer' and 'management' as the former (board of directors, elected members) may well have a different – and more progressive – position; indeed, in the case of elected members (as in local government), it may be the declared policy as set out in the election manifesto that will be your bargaining lever. However, it can be the other way round: 'management' (i.e. line managers and personnel officers) may feel an antagonism towards their superiors, and the union may be able to turn this to its advantage.

At all events, there will be at least as much campaigning as there was with the more recalcitrant trade union members. Sometimes it will be possible to make overtly political claims (the apprentices' contribution to thinking on local accountability in Sheffield, quoted by Martin Yarnit, p. 47). More often, the 'management arguments' of the type quoted by Workbase will be more likely to have an appeal for suspicious managers (p. 97). It might be added in this context that more liberal, progressive employers have noted with pleasure that staff who have attended basic adult education courses on PEL have appeared, on their return to work, quite simply to 'have more zest'.

When all is said and done, it's no use developing brilliant campaigns to persuade unions and managements to 'buy' the idea of PEL if the 'customers' are not interested. I have laid a lot of stress on the need to carry out careful and extensive face-to-face work with the potential students, but it will be of no avail if we have not approached, and overcome, the problem of *cover*.

'Cover' (see pp. 22–6 for an analysis of the problem) is the means of doing ('covering') the work that remains undone while the worker-student is away on her/his PEL study. Ideally, the problem is solved in one of two ways:

1 other members of staff do the student's work and get paid for the extra hours needed to perform this work;
2 students do the work themselves either before or after their study hours, and get paid for the extra hours needed.

The trouble with the former solution is that management will manoeuvre to get the other members of staff to do the student's work *in addition to* their normal work; the trouble with the latter is that management may manoeuvre to get the student to do her/his extra work during *other* normal working hours; a possible trouble with both is that some work (e.g. cleaning) can only be done at certain hours (for example, before other staff, students, teachers, etc. arrive to claim their offices and classrooms). Whatever the particular problems are, there is *no* chance of PEL getting off the ground if the problem of cover is not faced up to *and solved* before the lessons begin. A further difficulty is that the economic recession is forcing – or permitting – employers to reduce staffing levels, thus putting new strains on many groups of staff. The added threat (real or unreal) of putting the work out to contract (called 'privatization' in the public sector) strongly discourages workers to concede, however obliquely, that the work can be done at all with a smaller complement.

An exceptional employer in this context was the much-lamented Greater London Council: during the last three years of its life before its demise at the hands of the 1982 Tory government, it was agreed with the unions that all training *and cover* costs would come out of a *central* training fund. Apart from thus making it much more difficult for departmental management to impede training aspirations, this device also meant that the cost of the extra staffing hours necessary to cover the work left undone was borne by the employer *and* it minimized line management's opportunities to impose more work on the students, or otherwise deter them from taking part in the courses.

The courses, the anecdotes, the personal growth described in this book only happened, of course, as a result of an agreement with an employer. Nobody will imagine, I am sure, that employers are that eager to pay for PEL, so it is worth looking briefly at the tasks that precede these gladiatorial exchanges.

Practices vary enormously from one industry to another and from one part of the country to another; similarly, union rule books provide for widely differing modes of internal consultation. Notwithstanding, this nitty-gritty side of things might go something like this:

Stage 1 Branch discussion around a prospective claim for PEL; this discussion might have been initiated by the prospective students themselves, by a union activist *or* by the education co-ordinator (a new branch 'post' developed by a few unions, including NUPE and NALGO).

Stage 2 A small group of members get together separately to hammer out details of the claim: What areas of study? Who might be approached about attending? How would they be selected (no management cloning, please!)? What time(s) of the day? Venue? At this stage, it may well be advantageous to co-opt somebody from the adult education group that you want to do the course(s), ideally the person who will be involved in the outreach work.

Stage 3 The union presents management with a '*package*', a fully documented – and priced – proposal. (Intermediate stages of the procedure, e.g. involving line management, should be sidestepped, with the agreement of management.)

Impeccable advice! All the above is irrefutable really; but we plainly also need to grasp one or two other nettles such as: how do we speed up the process of getting more PEL courses going? how does the private sector get drawn into this? and what kind of entitlement, funding and control should be argued for?

12
Towards a national strategy

Jane Mace and Martin Yarnit

Most of the paid release projects described in this book have arisen from local initiatives. A firm, national approach to PEL on the part of some trade unions would open up wider possibilities. After all, despite mass unemployment, some groups of workers have retained their bargaining power. This seems to be the case in the NHS:

> Shortages of nurses, midwives, occupational therapists and other groups in the National Health Service, have led to the setting up of a working group to try to improve NHS career prospects for women.
>
> Mr Tony Newton, the Health Minister, anouncing the initiative, said the NHS was greatly dependent on its 750,000 women. Breaks in service to care for children should not leave women disadvantaged.[1]

In other words, there is probably more scope for developing the tactics suggested by Mike Cunningham in the previous section than seems to be the case at first sight. Even with the full backing of trade unions, this is likely to be a slow and uncertain process. Above all, it is unlikely to answer the needs of workers who are not unionized or who lack leverage even if they are. With the shift to part-time work in women's jobs and with the growth of employment in the service sector, particularly catering, retail and tourism, all industries where temporary contracts are becoming increasingly common, trade union bargaining power requires the backing of legislation to secure the right to paid release.[2]

Legislation is essential, therefore, if PEL is to become a common feature of private-sector employment, of small workplaces and of less powerful groups of workers, above all the low paid, of whom women and black people form the vast majority. It is vital for another reason, in unlocking educational resources and in altering the vast inequality in their distribution (see pp. 38–9, 44–5). 'Educational' here encompasses training, too, for a growing body of opinion in the trade unions and on the left now recognizes that we should be bidding for control over the content and distribution of the national training budget.[3] For political and organizational reasons, trade union education will remain the priority of the trade union movement; but surely it does not make sense for it to abdicate responsibility for the other 90 per cent of spending on education and training for adults?

A legal entitlement to education for all adults, in or out of paid work, would probably command a solid body of support today. How would it work in practice? What follows draws freely on the ideas developed over recent years by contributors to this book and others. We offer it as a basis on which could be built a coherent PEL strategy.

The first question concerns the nature of the entitlement, and how it should be paid for. The Merseyside PEL group in 1983 proposed a two-tier system:

1 a thirty-day per year entitlement to paid release, to be taken in a year or saved up and used in blocks (this would amount to a 'sabbatical' year every twelve years);
2 the right to longer periods of unpaid leave for higher education; but more courses would qualify for adequate mandatory grants to enable people to take time off from work without financial sacrifice.

The first tier would be paid for by the employer. Paid release beyond the thirty-day entitlement, complementary rights for the unwaged, and the second tier would be funded by the state.[4] The Labour Party has recently proposed the reintroduction of the employers' training levy, and part of this could be set aside for non-vocational education, perhaps along the lines of the Learning Development Fund proposed by Tom Schuller.[5] In this case, the costs of paid release (wages and cover) could be recouped by the employer from a central pool, as in the days of the training boards.

The second question, and a major concern for the trade unions, is what would this do for trade union education? Would it not simply fuel an expansion of vocational release or courses like those run by Workbase and Take Ten, where the balance of advantage between employer, employee and the trade union is often difficult to assess? A lot would depend on how seriously the trade unions took education, especially of the membership generally. The Merseyside PEL

Group proposed a local labour movement body to approve courses and promote paid release for workers' education. It would be a modified version of TUC regional education committees structured to ensure the representation of black people, of women, of the unemployed and unwaged. Serviced by the trade unions or local authorities, it would match demands and resources, playing a similar role to COU, the trade union education office referred to in Sonia Villone and Anna Brasolin's account of the '150 Hours' scheme in Bologna (see pp. 138 and 142). In Italy, and to a degree in Britain, such local bodies need to be underpinned by the groundwork carried out by workplace union representatives.[6] Highly localized promotion of PEL seems to be a constant feature of the most successful schemes in Italy.

COU, it should also be noted, has assumed responsibility not just for non-members of trade unions, but also for the unwaged in Bologna and the surrounding towns. The local education body proposed above could go a long way to rectify the trade union movement's neglect of unemployed people, particularly if it provided for direct representation of unemployed and community centres.

This still leaves some problems unresolved. First, how do you enforce the right to release? The Swedish system permits the employer to delay release by up to six months, and given full employment, and the power this gives to labour, this seems to be workable; but in Italy and Belgium workers are afraid to insist on their rights in case of dismissal.[7] Just as important as the right to release is the provision of cover, and that should also be dealt with by legislation and funding. Clearly legislation, even if backed by fines, as in Sweden, will not be enough alone to ensure enforcement. Still less can it overcome some people's reluctance to apply for paid release in the first place. A vigorous system of promotion and support may help, but again there is no guarantee of success.

This links to a second problem: the possibility that a minimum entitlement will be interpreted by employers as a maximum. This is the difficulty inherent in all social legislation, and unless the trade unions and other organizations sustain their commitment to PEL and make it a bargaining issue, it is hard to see a solution to this. Of course, the best organized will do better, but, at least, some of the less well organized will get something, and that will be a great deal more than they do at present. The parallel with holiday entitlement is interesting here. Improvements over the last forty years, as Mike Cunningham has pointed out elsewhere, have been accelerated by and combined with the overall strategy of the TUC and European trade union movements for a shorter working week.[8] This suggests two things: that employers *can* eventually come to terms with this kind of entitlement; and that linking PEL to a campaign for shorter working time could lead to pay-offs for both issues.

The third problem is who gets it. In the early 1980s, the Association for Recurrent Education (ARE) was widely influential with its campaign for a minimum educational grant for all (MEGA).[9] The idea was taken up by the Labour Party in its 1983 pre-general-election policy statement on post-18 education, and also by the Advisory Council for Adult and Continuing Education.[10] The notion of a universal entitlement is attractive, as long as there is some way of ensuring that the resources are targeted towards those who have fared worst with the education system. Local trade union education bodies and workplace education representatives could help. In addition, the legislation could set out the criteria for using the resources for PEL. In the end, though, a lot will depend on the strength of outreach and campaign work, and on the kinds of courses that are demanded and offered.

Notes

Introduction

1 The work of the Industrial Language Scheme (from 1969), however, did include courses for manual workers from ethnic minorities employed in some private industries. (See note 7.)
2 Sheila Lewenhak, *Women and Work*, London, Fontana, 1980.
3 John Killeen and Margaret Bird, *Education and Work: A Study of Paid Educational Leave in England and Wales (1976/77)*, Leicester, National Institute of Adult Education, 1981.
4 For information on PEL in other European countries, see: Alan Charnley's *Paid Educational Leave: A Report of Practice in France, Germany and Sweden*, Frogmore, Hart-Davis Educational, 1975; and Jean-Marie Luttringer and Bernard Pasquier's article, 'Paid educational leave in five European countries' (Belgium, France, Federal Republic of Germany, Italy, and Sweden) in *International Labour Review*, 119 (4). A comparison between Australia, Canada, Ireland and the UK in respect of PEL is to be found in Ian K. O'Malley's article in a later issue of the same journal (*International Labour Review*, 121 (2)). This is a brief survey and suggests the UK's legislation in terms of PEL for health and safety representatives' and shop-stewards' training puts it ahead of the other countries he studies (see our ch. 4, pp. 61–2). Arthur Gould's *Swedish Educational Leave in Practice: The Gothenburg Experience*, Nottingham, Association for Recurrent Education Discussion Paper 12, Spring 1984, offers an interesting summary of the work of the ARE in trying to make PEL a British campaign issue.
5 Our group failed to convene a conference; the Association for Recurrent Education (see note 4) was more organized, and in June 1986 convened a seminar at the University of Warwick on the theme of PEL. Particularly interesting papers were presented by Tom Schuller and John Field of the Department of Continuing Education, Warwick University (see notes 2 and 5 to ch. 11).
6 The expression was coined by the Swedish historian, Sven Lindquist, whose book of that title, *Grav dar du star*, was published in Sweden in 1978. Although this is not available in English, his account of how he set out to provide a practical manual for workers to write the history of their own workplaces is published in *Oral History Journal* 7 (2), Colchester, Oral History Society, 1979, 24–31.
7 English as a Second Language (ESL) courses for ethnic minority workers were run on a PEL basis by the Industrial Language Scheme, whose first

unit was set up in 1969. Since the 1976 Race Relations Act, the emphasis of their (now thirty) units across the country has tended, however, to be directed towards training management and personnel department staff in selection procedures designed to implement equal opportunities policies. Although this PEL work is outside the scope of this book, its indirect value for unemployed black manual workers is clearly important. (See address list for more information.)

Chapter 1 Paid educational leave: problems and possibilities (1976–86)

1 The report, *Why Should We have to Pay For It Twice?: Funding and Organising the Right to Study For Adults – Waged and Unwaged*, was published by the Merseyside Paid Educational Leave Group, 1983 (c/o Second Chance to Learn).
2 Cited in Philip Whitehead, *The Writing on the Wall*, London, Michael Joseph, 1985, 189.
3 See TUC, *Note of Comment on the Government's Consultative Paper, 'Education in schools'*, London, 1977, 2.
4 But see *Better Schools*, Department of Education and Science, 1985, 6.
5 John Killeen and Margaret Bird, *Education and Work: A Study of Paid Educational Leave in England and Wales (1976/77)*, Leicester, National Institute of Adult Education, 1981.
6 Killeen and Bird, 16, 35.
7 Advisory Council for Adult and Continuing Education, *Continuing Education: From Policies to Practice*, Leicester, ACACE, 1982, 70.
8 Julian le Grand, in *Strategy of Equality*, London, Allen & Unwin, 1982, 75, reported that professional and intermediate class candidates took nearly 70 per cent of acceptances of university places compared with under 20 per cent for the manual working class.
9 Manpower Services Commission, *Labour Market Report*, November 1985, 4.
10 See Labour Party, *Education after 18*, London, 1983.
11 David Parsons, *Changing Patterns of Employment in Britain*, Brighton, Institute of Manpower Studies, 1985, 10.
12 Jane McLoughlin, 'There's a bright future for those who want insecure jobs without perks', *Guardian*, 31.7.86. The survey, by John Atkinson and Nigel Meager, is called *Changing Work Patterns – How Companies Achieve Flexibility to Meet New Need*, London, National Economic Development Office, 1986.
13 Trevor Carter, *Shattering Illusions*, London, Lawrence & Wishart, 1986, 136.
14 Paddy Maguire *et al.*, *The Republic of Letters: Working-class Writing and Local Publishing*, London, Comedia, 1982, 2.
15 Liz Cousins, *I'm a New Woman Now: Education for Women in Liverpool*, Liverpool, Priority, 1981, section 10. There is also a checklist for course providers for working-class women.

16 Paulo Freire, *Pedagogy of the Oppressed*, Harmondsworth, Penguin, 1972; quoted in Judith Edwards, *Working-Class Adult Education in Liverpool: A Radical Approach*, University of Manchester, 1986. 3.

17 Martin Yarnit, 'Italy's experiment in mass working-class adult education', in Jane Thompson (ed.), *Adult Education for a Change*, London, Hutchinson, 1980, 199.

18 *Trade Union Studies Journal*, Summer 1986, 23.

19 *Social Trends 1986*, London, HMSO, 175–7.

20 See David Blunkett and Geoff Green's explanation in *Building from the Bottom: the Sheffield Experience*, London, Fabian Society, 1983, 26.

Chapter 2 Now or never: women, time and education

1 Sheila Rowbotham, who did us all a service in editing ten years' worth of her articles in *Dreams and Dilemmas* (London, Virago, 1983), has reflected: 'The early 1980s have pushed many of the discussions which during the 1970s took place in tiny groups, local meetings and single-issue campaigns in the women's movement out into a wider political arena.' (136)

2 Mary Hughes and Mary Kennedy, in *New Futures: Changing Women's Education* (London, Routledge & Kegan Paul, 1985), assembled a number of statistics which support this: 'In the British university adult education departments in 1978/9 there were only 12 women at senior lecturer level and above compared with 193 men. . . . In March 1983 the General Secretary of the Association for Adult and Continuing Education (AACE), Lucia Jones, estimated that 80 per cent of all part-time tutors were women as indicated by a survey in Croydon.' They cite DES figures which show that between 1976 and 1982 'women lost ground at senior management level', and 1978 research findings which show that in the local education sector there were nearly nine men to every woman at 'organizer' level (with responsibility for programme planning).

3 In *The Heart of the Race: Black Women's Lives in Britain* (London, Virago, 1985), Beverley Bryan, Stella Dadzie and Suzanne Scafe suggest one specifically female site where black women in the fifties and sixties chose to regather a collective strength in the face of relentless racial discrimination: 'The hairdressing salon, for example, served many Black women as a meeting place and more often than not the "salon" would be based in somebody's front parlour, since no European hairstylist would cater for our particular needs. Going along to have your hair pressed or rewaxed was a social event, an opportunity to meet and exchange stories with other women.'(130)

4 Amrit Wilson, *Finding a Voice: Asian Women in Britain*, London, Virago, 1978.

5 Barbro Hoel's essay, 'Contemporary clothing "sweatshops" – Asian female labour and collective organisation' in Jackie West (ed.), *Work,*

Women and the Labour Market, London, Routledge & Kegan Paul, 1982.

6 Figures quoted in CIS Report, *Women in the 80s*, London, Counter Information Services, 1981.

7 'Building businesses...not barriers', Cmnd 9764.

8 Bryan, Dadzie, Scafe, 119.

9 Nicholas Macdonald and Mel Doyle, *The Stresses of Work*, London, Nelson, 1981.

10 GLC, *Training for Change: the GLC's Equal Opportunities and Positive Action Training Programme*, Greater London Council, 1986.

11 See Jane Mace, *A Time and a Place: a Study of Education and Manual Work*, London, Lee Community Education Centre, Goldsmiths' College, 1985.

12 Listed in GLC.

13 *Employment Gazette*, October 1985, cited in *The Fact About Women Is...'*, Manchester, Statistics Unit, Equal Opportunities Commission, 1986.

14 As Jenny Beale, in her book, *Getting It Together: Women as Trade Unionists* (London, Pluto Press, 1982), puts it: 'In our society servicing other people's needs is regarded as women's work. The work is given low value. At home, it is unpaid; in a job, it is low paid. Because of its low value, men don't want to do it, so it remains women's work. Men's and women's work stay separated. The circle is complete.' (106). Lindsay Mackie and Polly Pattullo, in *Women at Work* (London, Tavistock, 1977) say this about training attitudes among employers in the distributive trades to their 'servicing' workers: 'The scarcity of training opportunities in distribution with these few exceptions for potential managers, shows how a complacent industry can somehow service its own needs but at the same time allow thousands of women to slip into and out of its employment without skills, prospects, or promotion.' (104–5).

15 It would be impossible to list here all the published writing by women who have attended Fresh Start courses, women's writing groups, and the like. There is certain value in women, embarking on such adventures, reading the poetry and prose that flowers from them. These are a handful of titles in print (since they are published by community presses whose addresses are not widely known, these are included in the list of addresses at the end of the book): *Shush Mum's Writing* (1978) and *Shush Mum's Writing Again* (1981), Bristol Broadsides; *I Want to Write It Down* (1980), Peckham Publishing Project; *Paper on the Wind* (1984), Queenspark Books; *Tip of My Tongue* (1980) and *Who Am I?* (1982), Gatehouse Project; *Creating Out Pasts* (1983) and *It Didn't Come Easy* (1984), Lee Community Education Centre; *Our Lives: Working Women* (1984), Eden Grove Women's Writing Group. Sue Shrapnel Gardener's *Conversations With Strangers* (Adult Literacy and Basic Skills Unit with Write First Time, 1985) offers a range of experience in writing development with women and men which is an invaluable resource. I have also found Adrea Loewenstein's account of teaching writing in a

Boston women's prison (in Bunch and Pollack (eds), *Learning Our Way: Essays in Feminist Education*, Cross Press, Boston, 1983) an illumination on how women writing from the inside out can support each other.

16 Founded in 1920, Hillcroft Women's College is the only national residential college for women. Funded by the DES, it runs one- and two-year full-time courses for women with few or no qualifications (with mandatory grants). It also runs a number of part-time day and residential courses. Areas of study include computing, economics, European history, history of art, literature, drama, psychology, social and political philosophy, social history, social policy, sociology and statistics. Study skills and career and educational planning are an integral part of the courses.

17 'Earthworms' was published in a magazine from this course, with a limited edition for the participants only. It is reprinted here with the permission of the authors: Colleen Langton, Esther Mayall, Janice Cooley, Norma Walker, Carolyn Clayton, June Melody, Jane Mace and Ruth Lesirge.

Chapter 3 Why training matters

1 Maureen Woodhall, *The Scope and Costs of the Education and Training of Adults in Britain*, Leicester, Advisory Council for Adult and Continuing Education, 1980, 12.

2 John Killeen and Margaret Bird, *Education and Work: A Study of Paid Educational Leave in England and Wales (1976/77)*, Leicester, National Institute of Adult Education, 1981.

3 Woodhall, 13.

4 I believe YTS is an exception to this rule.

5 John Eversley, 'Trade union responses to the MSC' in Caroline Benn and John Fairley (eds), *Challenging the MSC*, London, Pluto, 1968, 218.

6 Killeen and Bird, 53.

7 For example, the attack by Bill Morris, Deputy General Secretary, Transport and General Workers' Union, (TGWU), on the Youth Training Scheme ('YTS "unfair to young blacks"' in *The Independent*, 24.10.86) and the MSC's target for black recruitment ('YTS race monitoring' in *New Society*, 24.10.86).

8 MSC, *Annual Report 1984–85*, Sheffield, MSC, 1985, 19–20.

9 Woodhall, 16–17.

10 'When it came to mentioning the names of companies that did this, only household names came to mind. "...market forces have not produced such a benign result".' 'Bridge that gap', *Guardian*, 3.4.86.

11 Woodhall, 13.

12 Sheila Marsh, 'Women and the MSC' in Benn and Fairley, 153.

13 MSC, 37.

14 Concerns voiced by TASS, amongst others: *TASS on Training*, London, TASS, 1982, 5.

15 Report by Central Policy Review Staff, HMSO.

16 Equal Opportunities Commission, *New Styles of Training for Women: An Evaluation of South Glamorgan Women's Workshop*, Manchester, EOC, January 1986, 11.
17 Equal Opportunities Commission, *Annual Report 1982*, Manchester, EOC, 1982; South East Regional Council TUC, *What's In It For Us – Women and the Alternative Economic Strategy*, London, SERTUC, 1983.
18 Helen Rainbird, 'New technology and training – union strategies towards occupational change', Institute for Employment Research, University of Warwick (unpublished paper), 1986, 11.
19 See Sheila Marsh in Benn and Fairley, 165.
20 ibid., 166.
21 Unemployment Unit, *MPs' briefing*, 24.6.86, 2. Only a minority of CP places include any training. Employers have to provide all overheads, including training, from a capitation payment of £440, unchanged since the scheme began.
22 MSC, 19.
23 20 per cent of women in part-time personal service jobs had a higher valued full-time job ten years earlier, according to a national survey quoted in: Sheffield City Council Employment Department, *Part-timers: The Hidden Workers*, Women in Sheffield no. 3, May 1984, 5.
24 'Ethnic origin and economic status' in Department of Employment *Gazette*, December 1985, quoted in *Labour Research*, London, Labour Research Department, February 1986, 3.
25 'How well are councils tackling race jobs bias?', in *Labour Research*, London, Labour Research Department, May 1986, 11.
26 ibid., 12.
27 Ann Pollert, 'The MSC and ethnic minorities' in Benn and Fairley, 188.
28 ibid., 178.
29 Sheila Marsh, seminar notes for London Council of Voluntary Organizations conference, 'Time for education and training', London, March 1986 (unpublished).
30 The Manor scheme is outlined in the civic newspaper, *Sheffield Today*, Publicity Dept, Town Hall, Sheffield, October 1986, 5.
31 Haringey Women's Employment Project, *Women and Privatisation: School Meals in Haringey*, London, HWEP, 1986.
32 Helen Roberts, 'Don't brush us underneath the carpet', in *Women and Training News*, (sponsored by MSC, published by Women and Training Group, GLOSCAT, Gloucester), summer 1986, 4.
33 Bradford Metropolitan District Council, *Changing Face of Bradford – District Trends 1984*, Bradford, 1984, 17.
34 EOC, *New-Styles of Training*, 11.
35 Ruth Aylett, in 'Women and computing in Sheffield City Polytechnic', argues for a vigorous publicity drive towards girls and older women to offset a marked fall-off in women's interest in computing: Sheffield, June 1986 (unpublished paper).
36 The Centre aims to recruit unemployed people with few or no academic qualifications, 50 per cent of whom are women, 40 per cent of whom are

black, and 70 per cent of whom are Camden residents. Interview with Centre manager, July 1986.

37 See the section on the education support unit in the Centre's *Annual Report, 1984–85*, London, Camden Training Centre, 1985.

38 Labour Research Department, *Labour Research*, London, LRD, December 1985, 310.

39 House of Commons Employment Committee, *Second Annual Report*, March 1986, vii.

40 See *Financial Times*, 16.6.86.

Chapter 4 Time off and trade union education

1 See for example, Gloria L. Lee, *Trade Unionism and Race: A Report to the West Midlands Regional Council of the Trades Union Congress*, Birmingham, 1984. 'A recurring theme in discussions with black members is their lack of confidence in trade unions to take their grievances seriously and for officials to represent them as readily or as effectively as they would a white person.'(6)

2 Aims of Stage I, union representatives' course, *Guide to TUC Education*, London, TUC, 1984, 12.

3 This statement, and following ones, from trade union students, are taken from transcripts of interviews with students on WEA/TUC courses in the West Midlands during January-March 1986. They formed part of an evaluation project undertaken by the WEA and we would like to acknowledge the help of all those tutors, students and researchers who took part.

4 *We Are Driven*, video available from Coventry Workshop, 38 Binley Road, Coventry.

5 These organizations all provide cheap, well-researched and available pamphlets of interest to trade union students: Labour Research Department, 78 Blackfriars Rd, SE1 8HF; Low Pay Unit, 9 Upper Berkeley St, London W1H 8BY; Child Poverty Action Group, 1 Macklin St, London WC2B 5NH; Work Hazards Group, BSSRS, 9 Poland St, London W1.

6 A.J. Corfield, *Epoch in Workers' Education*, London, WEA, 1969, 133, quoting a 1965 report by A.H. Thornton and Fred Bayliss.

7 See Corfield (134–5) and Jack Jones, *Union Man*, London, 1986, 147.

8 'Memorandum of Evidence to the Royal Commission on Trade Unions and Employers' Associations; submitted by D F Bellairs, Senior Lecturer in Trade Union Studies, Slough College. 31 March 1966.

9 *Royal Commission on Trade Unions and Employers' Associations 1965–1968, Report*, London, HMSO, 1968, paragraph 712: 'Additional resources are undoubtedly required. These should be used to develop competent teachers and adequate syllabuses with a view to using training of stewards as part of a planned move to more orderly industrial relations based on comprehensive formal factory or company

agreements. This is where shop steward training will be able to make its biggest contribution.'

10 *In Place of Strife*, *A Policy for Industrial Relations*, London, HMSO, 1969, paragraph 76: 'A reform of the collective bargaining system will make it even more necessary than it is now that trade union officers at all levels, full time and voluntary, should be well trained. The Trade Union Development Scheme will be able to help with the cost of new courses provided by the TUC and the unions.'

11 Commission on Industrial Relations, Report no. 33, *Industrial Relations Training*, London, HMSO, 1972, paragraph 4: 'Training is an integral and essential part of the process of change in industrial relations.'

12 The Gold Report, the report of a working party on shop-steward education and training, Further Education circular letter 9/72, DES.

13 TUC policy on shop-steward education is developed in *Training Shop Stewards*, London, TUC, 1968, and in annual *Reports* to the TUC. Much of the information here comes from *Review of Trade Union Education Services*, Annex to Section F, General Council's Report to the 1975 Congress, London, TUC, 1975.

14 Details of DES/DE grant to the TUC are contained in 1976 and subsequent TUC *Reports*.

15 Rights to paid time off for trade-union representatives are now contained in the 'Employment Protection (Consolidation) Act 1978' sections 27 and 28, and in 'Code of Practice 3', London, HMSO, 1977.

16 See TUC *Reports*.

17 In the year ending March 1984, a £200,000 grant was made available for 'courses specifically endorsed by employers as being relevant to shop stewards' workplaces and of benefit to good industrial relations and health and safety'. (*TUC Report*, 1984).

18 Trade union journals are a good source of information about new courses and educational initiatives within that union.

19 See back issues of *Trade Union Studies Journal*, published twice yearly by the Workers' Educational Association. Issue 12 lists some of the relevant articles. (See especially, Joyce Brown, John McIlroy and Bruce Spencer, 'Fundamental questions about student centred learning' in *TUSJ* 7, 45–54). See also issues of *The Industrial Tutor*, journal of the Society of Industrial Tutors, particularly C. Edwards *et al.*, 'Student centred learning and trade union education: a preliminary examination', in *IT*, Autumn 1983, 4.

20 Dave Peers and Beryl Richards, *Say It With Video*, London, Comedia and the WEA, 1986, 23.

21 Articles by Lars Karlsson in *Trade Union Studies Journal*, 11 (18) and 12 (17).

Chapter 5 Paid or unpaid workers? Unemployment and release

1 Comments to the author by a woman unemployed centre activist, Merseyside, November 1986.

2 Remarks by a male unemployed centre activist during a meeting of the Merseyside Unemployed Centre's Co-ordinating Committee, October 1986.
3 Russell Report, *Adult Education: A Plan for Development*, London, HMSO, 1973.
4 ACACE, *Protecting the Future for Adult Education*, Leicester, Advisory Council for Adult and Continuing Education, 1981.
5 ACACE, *Continuing Education: From Policies to Practice*, Leicester, ACACE, 1982,
6 WEA, *WEA Manifesto: Work With the Unemployed*, London, Workers' Educational Association, 1981.

Chapter 6 Adult literacy: campaigns and movements

1 The class session at 'Anycity Literacy Centre' is based on an evening at the Lee Community Education Centre, Goldsmiths' College, London. The story is based loosely on one session in May 1986. All the names are fictitious, but the roles they played in this discussion are based on the group I was with that particular evening.
2 Peter Clyne's *The Disadvantaged Adult*, London, Longman, 1972, has been said to be influential in the production of the Russell Report, *Adult Education – a Plan for Development*, London, HMSO, 1973. This followed a number of government commissions of enquiry which, in the late 1960s, were recording a 'rediscovery of poverty', particularly in the inner cities.
3 *A Right to Read*, London, British Association of Settlements, 1974, 22.
4 Circulars on the subject from the then TUC General Secretary, Len Murray, in August and November 1975, followed by a third in April 1976, were addressed to Trades Councils, County Associations of Trades Councils, and TUC Regional Councils (circulars no. 184, 74/5, 34 and 145, 75/6).
5 Quoted in *Literacy at Work* (conference transcript), London, National Committee for Adult Literacy, October 1975.
6 Dougie Grieve, 'The adult literacy campaign' in *Labour Research*, London, February 1978, 46–7.
7 Our efforts achieved some column inches in the *Guardian* of October that year headed 'Literacy campaign "needs unions"' with this bold opening: 'Adult literacy tutors and students are launching a campaign to involve trade unions in helping workers who have difficulty with reading and writing. They fear that many teaching schemes are going to collapse or be trimmed back through lack of financial support when the Government-funded Adult Literacy Resource Agency is wound up in March. They feel that there are practical ways in which unions could step in to assist their members. . . . The conference will be told that the Government-backed campaign of the last three years has reached only 100,000 out of the 1 million people thought to need help.'
8 The three quotations are from reports in: the *Wakefield Express*

(17.9.76), the *Reading Evening Post* (28.7.76), and the *London Evening News* (20.1.75).

9 The Adult Literacy Resource Agency (ALRA) was established in 1975, to disburse the first government money directed at stimulating an improved adult literacy provision in this country. Renamed, with a new brief, as the Adult Literacy Unit (ALU) in 1978, it remained, essentially, a quango responsible for disbursing monies across the country for training programmes and new initiatives in adult literacy work. The Adult Literacy and Basic Skills Unit (ALBSU) was established in 1980, to succeed the Unit, and to continue to provide a central focus for 'adult literacy and basic skills work' in England and Wales. In each case, the Agency and the Units which succeeded it were part of the structure of the National Institute of Adult and Continuing Education. In this chapter, each of these is referred to at different points in the story. In a sense, it is one agency with two changes of name and, over time, changes of emphasis, receiving and disbursing funds direct from the Department of Education and Science and the Welsh Office. (Scotland has developed literacy funding and provision within its own structures.)

10 Quoted from the article ('Writing and its place in literacy work') that Alison Chapman and I wrote of the weekend, published in the *Adult Literacy Resource Agency Newsletter*, May 1977.

11 Marietta Clare, *The Adult Literacy Campaign: Policies and Practices*, stencilled occasional paper, Centre for Contemporary Cultural Studies, University of Birmingham, July 1985.

12 *Write First Time* (10), 1, Nottingham, March 1985, 1. This, and any other back copies of the paper, are available from: Avanti Books, 1 Wellington Rd, Stevenage, Herts, SG2 9HR. For further discussion of Write First Time's work see: Dave Morley and Ken Worpole (eds), *The Republic of Letters: Working-class Writing and Local Publishing*, London, Comedia, 1982, 125–8; Sue Shrapnel Gardener's *Conversations with Strangers*, Write First Time and the Adult Literacy Basic Skills Unit, London, 1985. Maureen Cooper's diploma thesis, 'Managing the collective Write First Time collectively – an examination of the necessary conditions: "every meeting an educational process"', Department of Extra-Mural Studies, University of London, is less easy to get hold of, but a valuable analysis.

13 Isobel Bowie's *Through the Door* was published by Blackfriars Literacy Scheme, Blackfriars Settlement, London, in 1982, but is now out of print.

14 *Listening Ears: Writings About the Education System*, Blackfriars Literacy Scheme and Cambridge House Literacy Scheme, London, 1980.

15 This and other conference reports available from: the National Federation of Voluntary Literacy Schemes, 131 Camberwell Road, London SE5 OHF.

16 See George Black and John Bevan, *The Loss of Fear: Education in Nicaragua Before and After the Revolution*, Nicaragua Solidarity Campaign/World University Service, London, July 1980.

17 Jane Lawrence, *It Used to be Cheating: Working Together in Literacy Groups*, National Extension College, Cambridge, 1985, 51–62.
18 *Preparatory Courses: Report of the Training Services Agency/Adult Literacy Resource Agency Working Group*, 1978; and *Guidelines for Preparatory Courses*, August 1980, Manpower Services Commission. See also: *TSD Preparatory Courses in the 80s* (conference report), London, National Association of Teachers in Further and Higher Education/Association for Adult and Continuing Education, April 1981.
19 *Where Do We Go From Here?: Adult Lives Without Literacy* (11 authors), Manchester, Gatehouse, 1983, 25.
20 M.J. Clark, *Job Link – a New Approach to the Work Preparation Programme: a South East Region Policy Document*, Brighton, Manpower Services Commission, 1985.
21 From a report (no author named) published in the *Adult Literacy and Basic Skills Unit Newsletter*, London, ALBSU, March 1986.
22 *Signing Off*, 1985, is available for hire from Barefoot Video, 50 Brunswick St West, Hove.

Chapter 7 Workbase (London)

1 At the time of writing, a report on the history of Workbase is being prepared, to be published in 1987. Available from Workbase (see address list).
2 Project staff, *S is for Statutory Sick Pay: A Report on the NUPE Basic Skills Project 1979–1983*, available from Workbase (see address list).
3 Jane Mace, *Working With Words: Literacy Beyond School*, London, Writers & Readers, 1979.

Chapter 8 Take Ten (Sheffield)

1 The authors of the piece are: Iris Cowley, Barry Jowle, Alan Fields, Janet Crooks, Andrew McClements, Carmen Lawrence, Mick Parkin, Roy Greaves, Steve Pickering and Corinne Palmer.
2 For examples of this tradition see Jane Thompson (ed.) *Adult Education for a Change*, London, Hutchinson, 1980.
3 'Racism in the workplace and community' is a discussion pack published by the Learning Materials Service, Milton Keynes, Open University (no date).
4 We are aware that a ten-day course can only be a 'taster', and since Take Ten was set up, Derbyshire County Council has established a programme based on a much more substantial amount of release for council employees, which began in January 1985. The courses are structured in two parts, of twenty days each. Workers gain release not only for this but also for a further time in which to carry out research projects, between the first and the second part of the course, up to a maximum of ten days, and attend a residential weekend at Northern College for which costs are

met by the employer. (Further information can be obtained from the Department of Adult Education, University of Nottingham.)

Chapter 9 Second Chance to Learn (Liverpool)

1 The research on which this chapter is based was carried out by a group of students on Second Chance to Learn. Without their work, designing questionnaires, conducting and writing up interviews and analysing the data, this chapter would not have been written. We are indebted to Anthony Crawford, May Evans, Bessie Hall, Ann Helsby, May Martin, Lin Parker, Mike Pines, and Maureen Reason, and to the ex-students who completed the questionnaires and agreed to be interviewed.

2 See Judith Edwards, *Working Class Adult Education in Liverpool: A Radical Approach*, Manchester Monographs, Manchester, 1986; and Martin Yarnit, 'Second Chance to Learn, Liverpool: class and adult education' in Jane Thompson (ed.), *Adult Education for a Change*, London, Hutchinson, 1980. See also Liz Cousins, *I'm a New Woman Now: Education for Women in Liverpool*, Liverpool, Priority, 1981; and *Second Chance to Learn: Education for Change*, report of first national conference of Second Chance courses, Liverpool, November 1983, Liverpool, Institute of Extension Studies, 1984.

Chapter 10 150 Hours (Bologna, Italy)

1 Not very much is available in English on the '150 Hours' scheme in Italy, least of all written, as this chapter has been, from first-hand experience of its practice. The following, however, offer some further reading ideas: Lesley Caldwell, 'Courses for women: the example of the 150 Hours in Italy', in *Feminist Review*, no. 14, June 1983; Colin Titmus, in his *Strategies for Adult Education: Practices in Western Europe*, Milton Keynes, Open University Press, 1981, devotes a chapter to the scheme's history (203–16); M. Risk and B. Crossman, 'The right to continuing education and the Italian initiative', *Adult Education*, vol. 52, no. 4, November 1979; and Martin Yarnit, 'Italy's experiment in mass working-class adult education' in Jane Thompson (ed.), *Adult Education for a Change*, London, Hutchinson, 1980.

Available in English is an overview of the programme, published in 1983, entitled *Adult Education in Italy: Research and Experimentation*, published by the Centro Europeo dell'Educazione (CEDE), Villa Falconieri, 00044 Frascati (Roma), Italy.

2 Effectively, that is, because Italian schools traditionally refuse the right to take the end-of-year exam to pupils who are unlikely to pass it. So, in practice, those who do sit it tend to be successful. The 150 Hours in Bologna and elsewhere take this a step further: sitting means passing.

Given the weight attached to continuous assessment, sitting the exam is very much a formality.

Chapter 12 Towards a national strategy

1 'NHS boost for women', in the *Guardian*, London, 19.12.86.
2 John Field, in 'What workers, what leave? Changing patterns of employment and the prospects for PEL', unpublished paper for the Association of Recurrent Education Conference, Warwick University, 13.6.86, sets out the major employment shifts which need to be taken into account in developing a PEL policy.
3 John Field.
4 Merseyside PEL Group, *Why Should We Have to Pay for it Twice?*, Liverpool, Merseyside PEL Group, April 1983.
5 Tom Schuller, 'Paid educational leave: idée passée or future benefit?', unpublished paper, Department of Continuing Education, Warwick University, September 1986.
6 See the survey of developments in Vauxhall/Bedford, ICI and British Telecom in Labour Research Department, *Bargaining Report*, February 1986, 10–11.
7 International Federation of Workers' Educational Associations, *Paid Educational Leave – A New Social Right*, report of an international seminar held in Dublin, November 1981, IFWEA, 9 Upper Berkeley St, London W1, 1983, 20.
8 Michael Cunningham, *Non-wage Benefits*, Pluto, London, 1981.
9 Arthur Gould, *Paid Educational Leave, Educational Leave, Grants and Awards*, Nottingham, Association for Recurrent Education, 1979.
10 Labour Party, *Education after 18: Expansion with Change*, London, Labour Party, 1983; and ACACE, *Continuing Education: from Policies to Practice*, Leicester, ACACE, 1982.

Addresses

Further information about courses is available from your union and from the Trades Union Congress regional education officer. A source of general information and debate is *The Trades Union Studies Journal*, from the Workers' Educational Association or the Trades Union Congress (addresses below). Note 5 to chapter 4 includes some other useful addresses.

ACACE, c/o National Institute of Adult Continuing Education, 19b de Montfort Street, Leicester LE1 7GE
Adult Literacy and Basic Skills Unit, 229 High Holborn, London WC1
Association for Recurrent Education, c/o Centre for Research into the Education of Adults, Cherry Tree Buildings, University of Nottingham, Nottingham NG7 2RD
Bristol Broadsides, 108c Stokes Cross, Bristol BS1 3RU
British Association of Settlements, 13 Stockwell Road, London SW9
Eden Grove Women's Writing Group, c/o AEI Department, Ring Cross Junior School, Georges Road, London N7
Gatehouse Project, St Lukes, Sawley Road, Miles Platting, Manchester M1 3LY
Labour Research Department, 78 Blackfriars Road, London SE1 8HF
Lee Community Education Centre, 1 Aislibie Road, London SE12 8QH
Merseyside Trade Union Community and Unemployed Resource Centre, 24 Hardman Street, Liverpool L19 AX
National Centre for Industrial Language Training, Havelock Centre, Havelock Road, Southall, Middlesex UB2 4NZ
National Extension College, 18 Brooklands Avenue, Cambridge CB2 2HN
National Federation of Voluntary Literacy Schemes, Cambridge House, 131 Camberwell Road, London SE5 OHF
Queenspark Books, 13 West Drive, Brighton
Second Chance to Learn, Harrison Jones School, West Derby Street, Liverpool 7
Take Ten, Philadelphia Centre, West Don Street, Sheffield S6 3BH
Trades Union Congress, Great Russell Street, London WC1
Workbase, Southwark Institute, Hunter Close, Weston Street, London SE1
Workers' Educational Association, 9 Upper Berkeley Street, London W1
Write First Time, c/o Gatehouse (address above)

Index